Charlotte Fyfe was born near Marlow, Buckinghamshire and grew up in Oxfordshire. She attended Oxford High School and subsequently read Classics at London University. In 1986 she married Alistair Fyfe, a Major in the Royal Tank Regiment; they have three sons and live in Wiltshire. Charlotte is May Cannan's great niece and is the daughter of Christine Pullein-Thompson, whose mother was Joanna Cannan, the well-known novelist. This is Charlotte's sixth book.

THE TEARS OF WAR

May, the daughter of Charles Cannan, Dean of Trinity College, Oxford, met Bevil, the son of Sir Arthur Quiller-Couch, when he came up to Trinity in 1910. When war broke out in 1914, Bevil was sent to France to serve as an Officer in the Royal Artillery. Within days of the Armistice, Bevil asked May to marry him — but tragedy struck. Here is the couple's story told through May's published poetry, with passages from her autobiography and letters from Bevil and his father, interspersed with official war diary extracts. It is a moving account of the melancholy of a war which stole the lives and loves of a generation.

Edited by
CHARLOTTE FYFE

---◆---

THE TEARS
OF WAR

The Love Story of
a Young Poet and a War Hero

May Cannan
Bevil Quiller-Couch

Complete and Unabridged

ULVERSCROFT
Leicester

First published in Great Britain in 2000 by
Cavalier Books
Upavon
Wilts

First Large Print Edition
published 2001
by arrangement with
Cavalier Books
Upavon
Wilts

Cover design by Nancy Lawrence

British Library CIP Data

Cannan, May
    The tears of war.—Large print ed.—
    Ulverscroft large print series: non-fiction
    1. Cannan, May 2. Quiller-Couch, Bevil
    3. Women poets, English—20th century—Biography
    4. Poets, English—20th century—Biography
    5. Large type books
    I. Title
    821.9′12

    ISBN 0–7089–4602–X

Published by
F. A. Thorpe (Publishing)
Anstey, Leicestershire

Set by Words & Graphics Ltd.
Anstey, Leicestershire
Printed and bound in Great Britain by
T. J. International Ltd., Padstow, Cornwall

This book is printed on acid-free paper

Lamplight

We planned to shake the world together, you
and I
Being young, and very wise;
Now in the light of the green-shaded lamp
Almost I see your eyes
Light with the old gay laughter; you and I
Dreamed greatly of an Empire in those days,
Setting our feet upon laborious ways,
And all you asked of fame
Was crossed swords in the Army List,
My Dear, against your name.

We planned a great Empire together, you
and I,
Bound only by the sea;
Now in the quiet of a chill Winter's night
Your voice comes hushed to me
Full of forgotten memories: you and I
Dreamed great dreams of our future in
those days,
Setting our feet on undiscovered ways,
And all I asked of fame
A scarlet cross on my breast, my Dear,
For the swords by your name.

We shall never shake the world together, you
and I,
For you gave your life away;
And I think my heart was broken by the
war,
Since on a summer day
You took the road we never spoke of:
you and I
Dreamed greatly of an Empire in those
days;
You set your feet upon the Western ways
And have no need of fame —
There's a scarlet cross on my breast, my
Dear,
And a torn cross with your name.

Acknowledgements

I wish to express my deep gratitude to Jim Slater, May Cannan's son, without whose help this book would never have originated. Jim Slater holds the copyright for May Cannan's poems and for her autobiography, *Grey Ghosts and Voices*. I would also like to thank Guy Symondson for kindly granting permission for me to quote from Bevil's and Q's letters; for taking me to Fowey and showing me The Haven and for all his assistance in answering questions (Guy Symondson is Q's great nephew). I would also like to thank my mother, Christine Pullein-Thompson for her help and advice and her sister Diana for providing photographs of May and her sisters, Dorothea and Joanna Cannan. (The Pullein-Thompson sisters: Josephine, Diana and Christine are daughters of Joanna Cannan). And lastly I would like to thank my husband, Alistair for all his support and help with the military side of the book.

Foreword

In November 1998 I bought a copy of *Poems of the Great War*, a little book published by Penguin to commemorate 80 years since the Armistice of the First World War. I was delighted to see one of my great aunt, May Cannan's poems, *Lamplight*, had been chosen for the book. This made me think how wonderful it would be to republish a selection of her poems. I already had one volume, *The Splendid Days*, published by Blackwell in 1919, and my mother sent me *In War Time* (1917) and *The House of Hope* (1923). I also had a copy of *Grey Ghosts and Voices*, May Cannan's autobiography which was published in 1976, three years after her death. I wrote to Jim Slater, May's only son, my second cousin and asked for permission to republish. He was delighted and immediately sent me some of her unpublished verses and photographs. I knew that May and Bevil Quiller-Couch, the son of Sir Arthur Quiller-Couch, had become engaged shortly after the war ended and that he had died tragically in the great flu epidemic of 1919. Now I wanted to know more. I asked for photographs of Bevil and also for more information on Charles Cannan, May's father and my great grandfather. He had been Dean of Trinity College, Oxford, an Aristotelian scholar and Secretary to the Delegates of the Oxford University Press. Thereafter a number of parcels started to arrive. I had all the information I needed to produce a book.

After Bevil died, May typed up every letter he had written home to his parents. She also typed up all the letters sent by his fellow officers to Sir Arthur Quiller-Couch after his death. In 1919 she had also typed up her own copy of the official War Diaries for all the formations in which he had served. Everything had been kept in wonderful condition by Jim Slater, and I even had a selection of original letters sent home from the Front by Bevil to May.

Since then the book has changed course. It is no longer only May's poems but it tells the couple's story through the poems, interspersed with extracts from May's autobiography and from Bevil's letters to May and to his parents. There are also extracts from the official War Diaries and quotes from Q's letters to his son and to May for whom he had a great affection. Lastly I have added some of May's unpublished poems which help tell her story and which she left in a handwritten notebook — these include: *The Ballad of the Sword*, *The Ballad of the Independent Young Woman*, *Riding*, *For Some*, *To the Germans*, *Now the Dawn Breaks*, *In Rome*, *In the Train*, *A Long Time After*, *The Echo 1923*, *For a Soldier*, *Perfect Epilogue* — *Armistice Day 1933*, and *The Long Road Home*.

Charlotte Fyfe

BEFORE THE WAR

May Cannan wrote in her autobiography, *Grey Ghosts and Voices*:

We were born, my twin sister and I, in a tall house in St Giles in the night of Saturday, 14th October 1893, the end of the first day of the Michaelmas Term. I have always liked to think that when I woke on that earliest Sunday of my life the air must have been full of the sound of Oxford bells. There was already an elder sister and it had been a son that had been hoped for; instead there were two girls. I do not think that either of us had much hold on life. We were not christened until December, and then in the house. The silver bowl that held the water says, 'May Wedderburn Cannan, Frances Kier Cannan,' and is silent. In the event, it was I who lived and Frances who died.

May grew up in Oxford, the daughter of Charles Cannan, Dean of Trinity College and later Secretary to the Delegates of the Oxford University Press. She was the second of three talented sisters. The family lived at Magdalen Gate House, a tall Georgian house in the High Street opposite Magdalen College, where May wrote:

We sat out and watched the moon coming up through the branches of an old apple tree. The garden smelt of wall flowers and lilacs and later on, of roses and stocks and Magdalen spoke the hours with his soft old voice.

May describes herself as short-sighted and clumsy; and she says she had a foreknowledge that 'life is a losing game'. She wept for all the sorrows of the world. Plain, plump, uncertain of herself, she says she spoke very little as a child. Her first words were reputed to be, 'Too many people', when her mother brought friends into the nursery one day. Her father's library was the room she loved best. 'At four I could read and had found my world'. She went to Wychwood School at eight years old along with her sisters, Dorothea and Joanna. Later, she and Dorothea were sent to Downe House School where May caught pneumonia and, probably because of this, returned to Wychwood to finish her education.

Life at Magdalen Gate House was always interesting. Famous writers were often found there — Kipling, T. E. Lawrence, Sir Walter Raleigh and Sir Arthur Quiller-Couch among them.

Sir Arthur, or Q as he was known, and Charles Cannan had both been educated at

Clifton College. Cannan was older than Q and it was Q who attended Cannan's lectures at Trinity College, Oxford. Charles Cannan became Secretary to the Delegates of the Oxford University Press in 1895, and, soon after, Q began working on *The Oxford Book of English Verse* for which he was the Editor and which was published in 1900. He was in fact the founder of the series of *Oxford Books of Verse*. Q was an all-round man of letters, writing short stories, novels, children's books and some verse. In 1910 he was knighted and in 1912 became the second King Edward VII Professor of English Literature at Cambridge and a Fellow of Jesus College so that, during the war, he spent much time travelling between Fowey and Cambridge. Of the novels that he wrote, one of his most famous, *The Astonishing History of Troy Town* was dedicated to Charles Cannan, who was practically a second father to him.

Q's son, Bevil, was born in 1890 and was named after the heroic Sir Bevil Grenville of the Civil War. His sister, Foy, was born in 1895 and named after Fowey. Bevil and Foy grew up at The Haven in Fowey in Cornwall. The Haven had been built by a naval lieutenant who had painted the name of a ship on each door and hung a water colour painting of each ship beside it (these pictures still hang on the doors today). Q and Bevil had inherited a love of all things nautical and Bevil had an idyllic childhood, learning to row at an early age and working on the 'Farm', which was a piece of land the Quiller-Couches owned on the other side of the harbour.

Magdalen Gate House, the home of the
Cannans in The High, Oxford
(by courtesy of Jim Slater)

The Haven, home of the Quiller-Couches, Fowey, Cornwall *(by courtesy of Guy Symondson)*

Bevil, Stroking for Trinity College
(by courtesy of Guy Symondson)

Bevil was educated at Winchester College; he was not an intellectual like his father but had more spirits that he knew what to do with. He took great delight in practical jokes as a child and later on at university. When he was about 13, he and his sister were left alone in the house while their parents and all the servants went out to a political meeting in Fowey. Bevil decided to play a game. The upstairs of the house was to be the sea and each room a port. Bevil blocked off the front and back stairs and let the bath overflow until there was about two or three inches of water over the whole of the upstairs floor. As the story goes, when their parents and servants came back, Bevil took away the barriers and the water came tumbling down the stairs to greet them. Subsequently, the drawing room and dining room ceilings fell down. A few years later, Bevil, while up at university, going through the turnstiles on Oxford station, found himself held up by an old lady followed by her black Aberdeen terrier. 'I happened to have a bag of flour with me and you should have seen the expression on that old lady's face when she turned round and saw her little doggie had gone quite white.'

Bevil possessed great personal charm, a sense of humour and was athletic. He had inherited his father's love of boats of every kind and in 1911 spent much of his summer holidays yachting either with friends or with the Commodore of Fowey Yacht Club, Edward Atkinson. Later on that summer he and Atkinson went sailing in a 12-foot boat off the coast near Fowey and the vessel foundered in heavy sea. Bevil managed to swim ashore to a small cove, supporting Atkinson who was unconscious. He left his friend on the rocks and went to fetch help, but before rescuers could arrive, Atkinson had been washed out to sea and, by the time the body was finally recovered, it was too late.

Bevil went up to Trinity College, Oxford in 1910 initially to read History but changed to Engineering after a year. He was there until the summer of 1913 but does not appear to have taken a degree. He was a first-class oarsman and rowed for Trinity College and for Oxford. Q said of him: 'I know he is one of the best four or five oars up at Oxford and I think he's easily the best stroke'.

It was at Magdalen Gate House that Bevil and May first met. Undergraduates were always dropping in to see Charles Cannan, even though he was no longer Dean of Trinity at this time. Bevil enjoyed the company of all three Cannan girls.

Bevil (top left) at Trinity College
(by courtesy of Trinity College, Oxford)

May wrote:

The Eight went to Henley Regatta to win the Ladies' Plate. Bevil was stroking her that year [1913]. We went on the last day and lunched with them all at Remenham Rectory among the water meadows, and drove home, when a thunderstorm had all but obliterated the fireworks, with the Quiller-Couches who were coming to stay.

While Bevil was at university in the three years before the war, the Cannans enjoyed climbing holidays in the Lake District, or mountaineering in the Swiss Alps. They were there each summer from 1911 to 1914. May and her family also spent time in Roshven in Scotland with relations. The Cannans had originally come from Scotland as had the Wedderburns on May's mother's side.

The Hills of Home

Moorlands purple and gold and brown,
Laughing burns that go dancing down,
Sun-kissed hills where the winds blow free,
Golden lights on a sunset sea;

11

Woods that are chequered with light and
shade,
Antlered heads in a forest glade,
Rowan trees in their scarlet pride —
Ah! Hills of home, but the world is wide.

Waters of Moidart clear and still,
Quiet shadows on moor and hill,
Mystical islands silver starred,
Golden sands by the grey rocks barred,
Creeks where the great tide eddies flow,
Green sea flowers in the depths below, —
O purple moors all dark with rain,
All hillmen come to their hills again.

Moorlands lashed with the sleet and hail,
Shrieked winds of a Northern gale,
Cruel waves all white with foam —
And the blown snow white on the hills of
home.
Road of the moorland winding away
Purple and gold and green and grey,
Over the pass and the windy hill
Where the wild moor creatures roam at
will,
And the red deer reigns in his royal
pride —
And down again on the Roshven side.

Waves that are breaking on golden sands,
Bringing a message from far-off lands,
Narrow ways where the tides run deep,
Seaweed isles where the grey seals sleep,
Lonely cliffs where the sea-birds cry —
And afar the hills of stormy Skye.

Whispering waves in the still lagoon,
A garden asleep 'neath a rising moon,
Jewelled isles in the blue loch set,
That we afar can never forget —
O hills of home, the world is wide,
But my heart comes home with the flow
of the tide.

May wrote:

Dorothea was 21 that November of 1913
and we gave a small dance in celebration.
Bevil came up and stayed with us for it and
she and he and I did most of the arranging
for it together. He had started work with
the Orient Line, called himself a 'city man'
and was taking an interest in politics. We
had some lively arguments for he was a
Liberal and I a Tory, and sometimes they
became heated, but we remained friends.
We went shopping together in the market
. . . and he gave us each a rose; a very sweet
gesture I thought . . . and long afterwards

he was to tell me that he had been secretly amused because I had described him earnestly to someone as a 'kind of brother'. He had, he said, for long had no intention of being or remaining one.

Romance

She stands in the water meadows,
She leans from the grey-lined walls,
She haunteth the great curved roadway,
She laughs in the college halls.
The joy of the West and the strength of
the North
Are written clear in her eyes,
And the love of the South hath made
them soft
And the lore of the East hath fashioned
them wise.
She stands in the sunset gardens
White robed 'neath a rainbow sky,
Till the shadows purple the velvet lawns
With the wind clouds driven by;
She leans from the towers at daybreak
Till the shadows have passed away
And the dawn creeps up from the
hill-tops
To herald another day.

To some it is given to find her,
Some kiss the hem of her gown;
To me it is given to seek her
Through the heart of her grey-spired town.
I follow her through her gardens
A daughter of distant kin,
Some day when I knock at the Gateway
Maybe she will let me in.
Till then I follow her footsteps
By meadow and street and lawn,
Hearing her pass in the night time
Hearing her voice in the dawn;
And dream that some April morning
At the turn of a darkling stair
I shall come out into sunlight
And suddenly find her there.

Oxford

Ever her children come and go,
Restless feet on her broad highways,
Ever her river runneth down
Blue and Green 'neath the alder sprays.

Ever her children come and go,
Joyful-hearted and ardent-eyed,
Ever she holds her hands to them,
Patient beyond all time or tide.

Ever her children leave her towers,
Echoing feet by night and day,
Ever her children come again —
O loyal hearts wide worlds away.

Ever she waiteth, sunset-fired,
Ever her river runneth down —
O weary feet from the ends of earth,
Come home at last to the grey-walled
town.

Dorothea Cannan
(by courtesy of the Cannan Estate)

Joanna Cannan
(by courtesy of the Cannan Estate)

May Cannan
(by courtesy of the Cannan Estate)

1914

May recorded:

They called it the Golden Summer afterwards, that last summer before our world came to an end . . . There were dances on those hot summer evenings, and picnics on the river . . . and Eights' Week with the boats going down to the start and deep voices calling 'touch her bow and two' . . . and then Term was over and there was the Magdalen Commemoration Ball. It was very nearly the end of our world. Magdalen, some say, is the most beautiful of all Oxford Colleges, and though it is always for Trinity that my heart turns over, I have kept through my life a great love for Magdalen living my early years under the shadow of her Tower; walking through the cool dark of her cloisters into the sunshine of the garden . . . Leaning over the bridge that crossed Cherwell to look for the flash of kingfishers' wings; wandering along Addison's Walk with my head full of poetry, thinking the long, long thoughts of youth . . . What I remember most of that last romantic night is the dew on the roses in the President's garden and saying goodbye in the dawn light in the empty street to my three best friends who were off that same day to camp. They were

20

going down, I think we all knew that we were saying goodbye, not only to each other, but to our youth. We went out to Switzerland.

Switzerland

There came to me a voice of wind and hills,
Crying, 'Come out! The faithful mountains wait,
And there shall be delight and all the state
Of battle night and day.

'And there shall be low laughter in the hills
And silences of snow-time and the sound
Of water lapping over thirsty ground:
These shall not pass away.

'And there shall be warm suns upon the rocks,
And the swift maddening music of hewn ice,
And lost endeavour for a sacrifice —
And dawn break into day.

'And there shall be blue skies against white snow,
And in the night a star above the pass;
And wide-eyed gentians in the upland grass
To speed you on your way.

'And in the end the quiet of lone paths
And the long shadows creeping down the hill,
And Alpine flowers upon a window-sill —
Twilight to comfort day.'

May wrote:

On 26th July, after some days of wandering about the mountains far removed from posts and papers, we bought a newspaper. My father immediately said, 'We must go home', and that night we caught the night express to Paris and crossed to Folkestone on 27th July. We had got home just in time. At midnight on the 4th of August England was at war with Germany.

May had already passed her First Aid exam and Home Nursing exams and, in the autumn of 1912, passed her Red Cross First Aid exam. In 1913 she had gained experience working in hospital wards. She was a member of the Voluntary Aid Detachment (VAD) which had been asked by the War Office to set up, in the event of mobilisation, a hospital and staff with 60 beds and provide a building. This was organised primarily by May and she managed to procure Magdalen College School for the purpose.

When war came, the War Office decided to close all VAD Hospitals and only use Military Base Hospitals. In the event Colonel Rankin, who did not have his Military Hospital ready, needed her hospital badly (the wounded were already arriving back in England) and it became an auxiliary hospital but to be staffed by military nurses. This meant that May and her staff were no longer required.

May wrote:

> I remember walking up the High on that autumn afternoon feeling very tired, too tired to be angry or resentful, and thinking only that it had all come to nothing, the thing that I had worked so hard for and to which I had given my heart.

Meanwhile May's friends were also preparing for the War. She wrote:

All my friends were in the Oxford University Officer Training Corps (OUOTC) or their Territorial Battalions at home, and some, like Bevil Quiller-Couch, who could spare the time when they went down, did six months training with the Regular Army and joined the new Special Reserve.

Bevil mobilised on the 6th August 1914, went up to Preston and took a draft of 80 reservists from there down to Aldershot the same day. He wrote home to his parents on the 8th August giving his address as 2nd Division Ammunition Column, Expeditionary Force, and said:

> England is doing quite well . . . the organisation has been splendid; every detail was ready in print five days after mobilisation was ordered — maps, stores, everything.

May wrote about Bevil and his mobilisation in her autobiography:

> On the 16th they were expecting to entrain the next evening: 152 men, 194 horses, 30 wagons, and three officers and on the night of the 17th a small Transport, SS Marchant, steamed quietly down Southampton Water and at 6am the next morning came into Le

Havre, and from thence went up the river to Rouen.

Meanwhile May's father saw his men from the Oxford University Press off to war — 63 men of the TA marched out on August 4th, and 293 enlisted in 1914 or later. May and her sisters were recruited to work as voluntary war-time staff at the Press. 'I shall need you all,' Charles Cannan told them. 'You had better come up to the Press.' They were intelligent, well-educated and could type and were better trained than most to understand their father's way of working. May worked tirelessly there on and off throughout the war and was given responsibility for putting together OUP's general catalogue.

May wrote:

I loved the place. I loved the coming and going, the dust and the smell of proofs with the printer's ink still wet on them; the darkness that spread from the windows on those winter evenings; the mounting tension as the end of the day came near and the post must go out . . . I knew I was happy. It was a great and learned Press and I was a very small cog in one part of it.

Charles Cannan, May's father
(by courtesy of Jim Slater)

26

August 1914

The sun rose over the sweep of the hill
All bare for the gathered hay,
And a blackbird sang by the window-sill,
And a girl knelt down to pray:
'Whom Thou hast kept through the
night, O Lord,
Keep Thou safe through the day.'

The sun rose over the shell-swept
height,
The guns are over the way,
And a soldier turned from the toil of the
night
To the toil of another day,
And a bullet sang by the parapet
To drive in the new-turned clay.

The sun sank slow by the sweep of the
hill,
They had carried all the hay,
And a blackbird sang by the window-sill,
And a girl knelt down to pray:
'Keep Thou safe through the night, O
Lord,
Whom Thou hast kept through the day.'

The sun sank slow by the shell-swept
   height,
The guns had prepared a way,
And a soldier turned to sleep that night
Who would not wake for the day,
And a blackbird flew from the window-
   sill,
When a girl knelt down to pray.

Bevil was with the Divisional Ammunition
Column during the Retreat from Mons, 23rd
August to 5th September 1914. The whole
British Expeditionary Force (BEF) had
crossed the channel and were gathered near
Le Cateau to the left of the French Fifth
Army. Both armies moved forward but near
Mons the British took the full force of Von
Kluck's 1st German Army. Outnumbered, the
British fought back but the French 5th Army
had started to retreat and, without their
support, the British were forced to withdraw
as well. However the British had temporarily
checked the German advance. As the BEF
withdrew, fighting constant rear guard
actions, they, under General Horace Smith-
Dorrien, became engaged, in the biggest
battle fought by the British Army since
Waterloo, at Le Cateau. Out of 40,000 men
there were 7,800 casualties. The retreat was
halted at the Battle of the Marne, 5th to 10th

September, when the BEF and French forces executed a counter-attack that caught out Von Kluck's 1st Army. Eventually the Germans withdrew. The Battle of the Marne was an important strategic victory for the Allies. Had they lost, the history of the 20th Century would have changed dramatically. The Marne remains, reputedly, the most decisive battle since Waterloo. Bevil fought at the First Battle of the Aisne, 15th to 18th September. The Allies succeeded in crossing the Aisne but were halted by the German resistance on the other side. Both the Allies and Germans began entrenching their positions and this was the start of static warfare on the Western Front. On 22nd September Bevil joined the 36th Brigade, Ammunition Column.

May wrote:

> I do not suppose that anyone who thought at all and who lived through the news of Mons could ever be quite the same again. I remember sitting on the porch steps that hot Sunday and being quite unable to speak. It must, I think, be true that one grows up in a sudden moment of time and experience, for I grew up on that day.

Bevil's Fellow Officers from the Battery (by courtesy of Trinity College, Oxford)

Gifts

Take you the sword,
The sword your fathers made for you,
Holding love and life itself things of little
worth;
Take you our hearts, our hearts that are
afraid for you,
Out to fight for England at the ends of
all the earth.

Take you our love
That shall unending live for you,
Out to hold the trenches in the
shell-tortured hours;
Take you our lives, the lives we may not
give for you,
Out to join the battle where your love
shall stand with ours.

Take you our dreams,
The dreams that we forsake for you,
Dreams of love and happiness we wove
in other days;
Take you our hearts, our lonely hearts
that break for you,
Out to bring you home again from
peril-haunted ways.

May was 21 in October. There could of course be no celebrations.

Bevil wrote to his parents on the 5th November 1914 — he had been at the bloody First Battle of Ypres:

The crisis is over now and it has quietened down. Never have I seen such fighting as on the 1st, 2nd and 3rd November. People may well be proud of the 1st Corps (that was Haig's) which held on for three days against more than treble its number of Germans. We have moved to a quieter spot and are now settled in a nice field with a farm close by with hay and straw and all necessities for the horses. We try and reassure the only people left behind, the old father and one of his daughters. She speaks French and in the rain last evening came out to offer us shelter in the house. I have not been under a roof since I joined this column and much prefer it. The other day, when I was riding alone, a shell came over the road in front of me. Some soldiers lay under the hedge when they heard it, but in the middle of the road was a girl wheeling a barrow of potatoes. She did not even trouble to look round but looked up and smiled as I went by. Pretty good that.

On the 11th November Bevil went up with six wagons of his Ammunition column to the 41st Brigade who were heavily engaged, and on the 12th he received a minor wound.

On the 13th November he wrote home again:

The news of the fall of German armies in Poland and the sinking of the *Emden* has cheered us up and after resisting the most desperate attacks for a fortnight we are full of confidence. I think Joffre has many cards up his sleeve yet and, now that he has slowly knocked all the heart out of them, we shall soon begin to move. 30,000 wounded passed through Brussels and Ghent in two days. Our Brigade did some grand work the other day, gunners with rifles and the guns firing at 500 to 800 rounds . . . Game is very plentiful now and hares and pheasants. A French Corps passed through here the other day and one of the Lieutenants showed me their field gun, the simplicity and the clever devices are marvellous. Their infantry were busy chasing hares with sticks and anything they could lay hands on, little men squatting in the turnips, one of them fell into a black muddy pond in a mad rush for a drowning hare, we all ached with laughing. Last night the wind and rain were phenomenal, I thought our bivouac would fly into the next field any moment but she held on like a brick and with a wall of turf sods round for walls we kept dry and snug. The farmer came over this morning and complained that there were two horses in his dining room and another in the lavatory which was no doubt annoying, they were not ours though.

Soon after Bevil had his first leave and went home to his family in Fowey.

May wrote:

The incredible move of our Armies from France to Flanders had been a race to save the Channel ports and at Ypres they had been saved. Heavy losses however were incurred [approximately 130,000 British and French troops]. It was a sad Christmas for everyone back home. There were too many soldiers who had already died.

1915

Bevil wrote his first letter to May early in 1915 and for the next three years they exchanged only a handful of letters. It was not until 1918 that their letters to each other became more frequent. Bevil wrote in his first letter:

Dear May,

It was great hearing from you and I hope you will write often ... Besides I don't think I have heard from you since I came out. But probably that is my fault as I have never written ... Things are very quiet now after the strenuous days of the Aisne and Ypres ... things were very fierce and I was so busy that it all seemed to rush by and I never had a moment ... Just a few hours' sleep in a pit with two blankets over me and one night I got covered with mud from a shell and never even woke up I was so tired ... I hope we shall be dancing together again this time next year.

Best of luck
Yours always Bevil

May recorded in her autobiography:

In March 1915 came Neuve Chapelle. Much had been hoped, but there were not enough guns, not enough shells, and there was the tragedy of the uncut wire. Hilary Raleigh [a friend and son of Sir Walter Raleigh] told me afterwards how, waiting till the barrage lifted and it was time to go over the parapet, a boy further along the trench turned suddenly and said, 'To die will be an awfully big adventure.' The time came — for a moment or two they ran together in No Man's Land, and then he fell.

May expressed the general feeling amongst those left behind that they wanted to be involved in the war in some way. She wrote:

All our hopes and all our loves, and God knew, all our fears, were in France; to get to France, if only to stand on her soil was something; to share, in however small a way, in what was done there was Heart's Desire.

May did go to France. She went to Rouen in the spring of 1915 and helped run the Canteen at the Railhead there for four weeks, serving the soldiers coffee and sandwiches. The time she spent at Rouen, the people she met and the things she saw inspired her most famous poem, *Rouen*.

Rouen

April 26 – May 25, 1915

Early morning over Rouen, hopeful,
high, courageous morning,
And the laughter of adventure and the
steepness of the stair,
And the dawn across the river, and the
wind across the bridges,
And the empty littered station and the
tired people there.

Can you recall those mornings and the
hurry of awakening,
And the long-forgotten wonder if we
should miss the way,
And the unfamiliar faces, and the
coming of provisions,
And the freshness and the glory of the
labour of the day?

Hot noontide over Rouen, and the sun
upon the city,
Sun and dust unceasing, and the glare of
cloudless skies,
And the voices of the Indians and the
endless stream of soldiers,

And the clicking of the tatties, and the buzzing of the flies.

Can you recall those noontides and the reek of steam and coffee,
Heavy-laden noontides with the evening's peace to win,
And the little piles of woodbines, and the sticky soda bottles,
And the crushes in the 'Parlour' and the letters coming in?

Quiet night-time over Rouen, and the station full of soldiers,
All the youth and pride of England from the ends of all the earth;
And the rifles piled together, and the creaking of the sword-belts,
And the faces bent above them, and the gay, heart-breaking mirth.

Can I forget the passage from the cool white-bedded Aid Post
Past the long sun-blistered coaches of the khaki Red Cross train
To the truck train full of wounded, and the weariness and laughter,
And 'Goodbye, and thank you, Sister', and the empty yards again?

Can you recall the parcels that we made
them for the rail-road,
Crammed and bulging parcels held
together by their string,
And the voices of the sergeants who
called the Drafts together,
And the agony and splendour when they
stood to save the King?

Can you forget their passing, the
cheering and the waving,
The little group of people at the doorway
of the shed,
The sudden awful silence when the last
train swung to darkness,
And the lonely desolation, and the
mocking stars o'erhead?

Can you recall the midnights, and the
footsteps of night watchers,
Men who came from darkness and went
back to dark again,
And the shadows on the rail-lines and
the all-inglorious labour,
And the promise of the daylight firing
blue the window-pane?

Can you recall the passing through the
kitchen door to morning,
Morning very still and solemn breaking

slowly on the town,
And the early coastways engines that had
met the ships at daybreak,
And the Drafts just out from England,
and the day shift coming down?

Can you forget returning slowly, stumbling on the cobbles,
And the white-decked Red Cross barges
dropping seawards for the tide,
And the search for English papers, and
the blessed cool of water,
And the peace of half-closed shutters
that shut out the world outside?

Can I forget the evenings and the sunsets
on the island,
And the tall black ships at anchor far
below our balcony,
And the distant call of bugles, and the
white wine in the glasses,
And the long line of the street lamps,
stretching Eastwards to the sea?

. . . When the world slips slow to darkness, when the office fire burns lower,
My heart goes out to Rouen, Rouen all
the world away;
When other men remember I remember
our Adventure

And the trains that go from Rouen at the ending of the day.

Philip Larkin chose this poem to be included in *The Oxford Book of Twentieth Century English Verse* (first published 1973). He wrote: 'found it in the Bodleian ... and immediately knew that this was something that had to go in. It seemed to me to have all the warmth and idealism of the VADs in the First World War. I find it enchanting.'

This is what May recorded in her autobiography about her experience in Rouen:

Along the length of railway line ran a row of sheds with huge sliding doors. In the first, and smaller one, was a boiler room where enormous vats of hot water forever boiled. Beyond, steps led to a room where we ate our own meals when there was time, and kept books for anyone who asked for something to read going up the Line. And across the whole of the great sheds ran heavy tables, ours with shelves under which at night held guttering candles and trays for change. Behind were the steaming cauldrons where we washed the unbelievably pink French bowls in which we served coffee and ham sandwiches. Once inside the gates there was never any trouble. Stumbling along in the dark one fell over groups of soldiers sitting or lying, rifles piled, waiting for their train to Railhead. Sometimes the yards were lit by the fires the Indians made, stirring their cook-pots, talking in strange tongues, and a tall bearded Sikh would rise up before one, or a merry-eyed Gurkha.

When the big trains were due in, we opened the sliding doors of the sheds, the train doors banged and banged down the long line of the corridors and some 2,000 men would surge in. Barricaded behind our heavy table, and thankful of it when the pressure was heavy or a draft had somehow got hold of some drink, we handed out bowls of coffee and sandwiches, washed dirty bowls till the water in the tall vats was chocolate brown, and served again. Some-one would play the piano; 'Annie Laurie'; 'Loch Lomond'. Blurred lanterns lit the scene as best they might when it rained and our candles in the tills under the tables guttered in the wind. One was hot or horrid cold, harried, dirty, and one's feet ached with the stone floors. When the smaller drafts came, one could distinguish faces, and regimental badges; have a word or two. Two men told me that they were

The New Army, Kitchener's! I said yes, and we had been expecting them, and thought of the old Army and the TA. Twice I came on an old friend but there was no time save for a brief greeting and a goodbye and good luck.

When the whistle blew they stood to save the King and the roof came off the sheds. 2,000 men, maybe, singing — it was the most moving thing I knew. Then there'd be the thunder of seats pushed back, the stamp of army boots on the pave, and as the train went out they sang Tipperary. Going up the Line to Railhead in that early Spring the drafts always sang it and it still brings back to me rain and blurred lanterns and men's voices dying away in the dark.

I Dreamed

I dreamed I stood alone in the white spacefulness which men call air.
There was no sound of speech or movement there,
But only my own quickened breath to hear,
And the vast voiceless silence everywhere.

Then through the empty archway of the sky
I saw an angel ride,
And as he rode he cried
'For England Victory.'
And all my heart went out to those who died
So that for all my pride
My voice broke tremulously.
And then I dreamed
He drew rein at my side,
The world was full of stars, his helmet gleamed,
(His eyes were like twin stars) almost it seemed
As if the moon herself hilted his sword,
And I could find no word.

I dreamed he spoke, and the stars leaning down
Made for him a great crown,
So that he stood in light,
And all behind was night,
Blue, unforgettable, unfathomable night.
His voice was as the voice of many waters, clear
And full of music as a violin,
Kind as the waves that lap a thirsty shore,
Deep with a million sorrows hid therein;

It was as if a blackbird sang
That the day might begin.

'Have you no answer then for me,' he
said,
(And bowed his bright head)
'No laughter though for joy they went to
die?'
Then I
Heard my voice break unnumbered miles
away
Upon the great roof of the world.
'Remember they
Gave of their best. Friendship they gave;
the love they hardly knew;
All the dear little foolish things of earth,
And all the splendid things they meant to
do;
Sunsets, and dawns, and grey skies
breaking blue,
All undiscovered worlds, and fairy seas,
And the lips of their girl-lovers. These
Gave Victory to the world, and Beauty
which is Truth;
And glad gay generous Love; the
unconquerable Love of Youth.
And I
How should I speak of Victory who went
not out to die?'

He spoke, and all the longing in the world
Broke in his voice, 'There came
Yesterday even unto Heaven's Gate
One from your war, and begged us leave to wait
For one who should come after, whom he called
'Comrade in Arms,' and smiled, and spoke your name.'

I dreamed:
And a moon-hilted sword lay in my hands it seemed.

The Bishop of Newcastle read *I Dreamed* to a crowded service in his Cathedral and was inundated afterwards by people wanting to know where it came from.

In May Bevil was in action at the Battle of Festubert (15th — 25th May) He wrote in his own hand in the War Diaries:

All the artillery bombard the German lines on and off all day. The 6th Infantry Brigade are reported to have made good the 1st German line by midnight. 71st Battery complete the wire cutting. 7th Division attack at 3.15am after an hour's intense bombardment. Attack successful and 1st line taken at the 1st Assault; infantry continue to advance by bombing. 250 prisoners taken, 71st Battery. OP[Observation Post] made untenable and wires cut. Artillery reopen bombardment at daylight in German lines. Reinforcements for Infantry. Guards and Canadians attack and consolidated on La Quinque Rue but attack on M 10 fails. Bombardment continues well into the night. 48th and 71st Batteries have now been firing an average of 600 rounds a day for about a fortnight without a break. Highland Division relieved 2nd Division. Just over 600 prisoners captured. Germans become very active and bring up much more heavy and light artillery. All the front and its neighbourhood heavily shelled ... Canadians attacked and consolidated a new position. Our trenches again heavily shelled. Continued wire cutting. Canadians attacked but had to fall back ... Much shelling. The German garrison cut off. Surrender at 8am. Operations are continued and in the middle, 36th Brigade is informed that it will be withdrawn together with the 41st Brigade at dusk.

A Ballad of June 1915

I made a garden for my love
With roses white and roses red,
And I must gather rosemary,
For my love lieth dead.

I planned to plunder all the stars
To make a chaplet for his head;
The rain beats on the window bars,
And my love lieth dead.

I meant to make a dream of days
With life by love and laughter led;
I stumble over stony ways,
And my love lieth dead.

I made a garden for my love
With roses white and roses red,
And I must gather rosemary,
For my love lieth dead.

Any Woman

The moon hath hushed the city,
The river runneth deep,

And I wonder where on God's green earth
You lay you down to sleep.

It is so still, the water laps
Low-voiced against the piers —
I wonder how the quiet lies
On tortured Armentières.

I wonder if you see the moon
Break blue on burnished steel,
Or if you sleep and wake to watch
The flaming lights of Lille.

Across the warm safe English fields
The sun brings up his day,
I live my life because in France
You give your life away . . .

There will be summer nights for me,
And poppies in the wheat —
O God, the bugles call so shrill
Across the empty street . . .

The sad stars pale, the dawn wind lifts
The roses on the wall;
Morning, and noon, and sunset-tide,
To you I owe them all.

Across my heart the shadows sweep,
As shadows come and go;

I'd give you all my world for thanks —
And you will never know.

May recorded:

> There was the heartbreaking long drawn
> out failure of the Dardanelles. Rupert
> Brooke was dead . . . There was Hill Sixty,
> Hooge and Loos — a dreadful battle
> among the mining villages with very heavy
> casualties. The German line was shaken but
> there was no real breakthrough.

Bevil wrote home in October 1915. This sort
of letter was typical of the kind of things
written home by men at the front who
emphasised the trivia and stressed the
positive so as to spare the feelings of those
they were writing to.

> I am so glad to hear the aunts in
> Hampstead have been visited by Zeppelins
> without causing apparently any alarm and
> despondency . . . We have moved at last to
> a very large empty house but there wasn't
> anything in it but bare walls and all the
> windows broken and very cold too.
> However we managed to rout around
> among the ruins and collect an excellent
> kitchen range (in which we roasted

grouse), a stove, three tables, two beds, 16 chairs and plenty of coal. We now have an open fire place in the morning room and dining room, all this goes on in the middle of what the Press call the greatest Battle of the War. The batteries are all just within 200 yards and one gun which fires just outside my bedroom brings down bits of plaster from the ceiling every shot. This is a pretty lively spot too and we are at it hard mostly all the 24 hours. We get the Bosche in the open occasionally which is a great target after a year in the trenches except for a fortnight at Ypres.

At the end of October 1915 Bevil wrote:

We are very busy now and I may have little time to write . . . the noise is deafening and we have had some of the house windows shattered but it is good to be stirring the old Bosche up again . . . this is war and no mistake; and it's grand to be out here . . . the German lines are like a furnace burning smoky coal; and the French are going at it like smoke too. The Brigadier is a great and splendid man. We had a shell into the middle of our breakfast two days ago but beyond blowing the Dixie eggs and bacon into the air no harm was done.

The Sloggers —Bevil (top left) at war (by courtesy of Trinity College, Oxford)

1916

January 1916

O Heart grown weary with the hope
that's fled,
Poor desolate heart that leans to
nothingness;
O eager hands reached out to meet
success,
Pity is killed and you have stones for
bread;
What will you do or how be comforted,
For all your prayers and all your soul's
distress
And all your agonies are powerless
To give you back one moment with your
Dead?

O lonely heart, take courage on your
way,
O empty hands, the world's work waits
your will;
Love shall endure being more than
mortal clay,
Death has killed Joy, but Hope remaineth
still,
Dawn shall bring dark, each hour an
hour until
Tomorrow slips star-shadowed to today.

Bevil Quiller-Couch was awarded the MC on 14th January 1916 and his citation in the *London Gazette* read as follows:

> Lieutenant Bevil Brian Quiller-Couch RFA SR. Exceptional ability and energy during the time he was with the Brigade Ammunition Column on the Aisne and in Flanders from 20th September to 16th of December 1914. On many occasions he showed great courage and initiative in bringing up his wagons. Since December in the Belhume District he acted as Orderly Officer until appointed Adjutant 10th June, 1915.
>
> He has shown great zeal and ability.
>
> During the recent active operations at Festubert and Le Plantin in May his services were particularly valuable. It was a great deal owing to his energy and grasp of the situation that everything worked successfully and smoothly. This particularly applied to the tactical control of the French Group and arrangements in connection with this Group generally.

The Battle of the Somme began on 1st July 1916. Bevil wrote home to say that he had been in action in what he supposed was one of the biggest battles of the war and:

The noise is deafening day and night without even ten minutes' peace . . . we are digging like moles . . . you should see me, black with dust and dirt, burnt with the sun and always hot.

Bevil had been promoted to Captain and joined the 71st Battery of the 36th Brigade on June 25th 1916, but on 15th August he was made Acting Major and given command of the 9th Battery, 41st Brigade, Royal Field Artillery, whilst still in action at the Somme.

May wrote:

The casualties at the Somme were terrible. Most of Kitchener's Army died there. It was said that Haig had wanted an offensive in the North but was told to follow the French Directive and they wanted one on the Somme where the two Armies joined. There were some limited gains but the Germans were too strongly entrenched and had too many machine guns. The battle went on and on, and ended in mud, water and death.

On the first day of the Somme casualties were 57,470 — the highest casualty rate in the history of the British Army — over 19,000

British were killed. The campaign lasted until 18th November and overall the British casualties were over 400,000.

Girl's Song, 1916

In heaven there be many stars
For the glory of the Lord,
But one most bright which is the light
Upon my true love's sword,
To show that he always for me
Keepeth good watch and ward.

In England now few lamps there be
Since Death flies low by night,
But brave behind the lowered blind
Shall mine burn steady bright,
That he may know for him also
Burneth a kindly light.

Bevil wrote home on 16th September 1916:

The Army in France is continuing to do great things ... the 9th Battery also continues to do great things in a small way and co-operating with the Infantry they secured 11 unwounded prisoners last night, killed two Germans and never had a casualty. The shooting keeps me busy all day.

Bevil had now been fighting in the war for two years. His letters home describe life relatively free from death and destruction but he was at great pains not to reveal any of the horrors of war, especially to his mother. Life, when Bevil's Battery was at rest and moved well back behind the lines, could seem positively idyllic: 'We have been having a splendid time these last few days and doing great things. The country is beautiful and the weather perfect. We are on a high hill with a flooded river which we look down on to. The floods have formed one large lake which has poplar trees standing up in the water and a glorious wood on the far hill'.

Bevil wrote home at various intervals for a fascinating array of things he needed. For example he wanted:

Cakes of Verbena or Gibbs soap at regular intervals and shaving soap
Pipes, matches and cigarette papers for the men
Socks
Khaki handkerchiefs and a khaki tie

Woolly under waistcoat and short thick
drawers
A new hat
Long leather bootlaces
A notebook for Bevil and books for the
Battery

And food was very important. He regularly
asked for:

Hoggy Pudding — This was Hogs Pudding, a Cornish version of Cumberland
sausage
Cakes
Tins of coffee

And for the horses and their equipment:

Saddle soap and Wren's paste
Steel horse comb to smarten the Brigade
Staff horses' manes and tails
A tooth rasp
A hunting snaffle with large rings

And slightly more unusual requests for head
ropes for the horses:

All mounted units are complaining of the
shortage of head ropes . . . My idea is that
you might write and ask if you [his father]

could form a small company of say 12 men . . . requisition rope and get it sent down . . . Head ropes are eight feet long with a ring spliced in one end and a Cape Horn whipping on the other; a squad, such as I suggest of old sailors, could turn out 100 per evening or more and send them by rail to Ordnance for distribution abroad. If you could arrange this officially, I am sure it would be of great help.

And for fly papers:

There is one thing badly needed at once and that is a large supply of fly papers. Can you send them out as there are already a good number of flies and, where the great battle raged round here in November and December, there are plenty of corpses left which were not covered too deeply by the French. Also many of the houses collapsed and buried many a Bosche as he stood when the French let off a series of large mines. The matter is being taken firmly in hand and we are all working at cleansing but everything should be done with this hot weather coming. The French seem to have done nothing in that way all the winter they were here.

May, like many other women of the time, believed that war was right and that her pain and loss, like that of many others, was for a greater cause. She did believe that men were sacrificing their lives for the good of their country.

On the Chilterns

We lay out on the Chiltern hills all day,
And watched the shadows sweep the clouds away
From Surrey, Berkshire, Hampshire, Buckingham.
The sun was blown to a red oriflamme,
September had kissed Summer long goodbye.
And then she turned to me and asked if I
When the time came, would be afraid to die;
Our eyes met and we smiled, she wondered why.

How should we be afraid when our loves led
Our hearts, oh long ago, half through Death's door,

Seeing that our most dear and faithful
Dead
Will mark the road for us they passed
before;
And since we miss them though our lives
are sweet,
Perhaps they'll be a little lonely too,
And when the door swings back we'll
turn to meet
The laughing-hearted friends that once
we knew.

Autumn, 1916

Late roses beat against the wall,
The swallows gather by the sea,
And Summer goes from England now,
A woman weeping bitterly;
O Summer crying, Summer sighing,
Ease you of your pain,
For all your tears the barren years
Will not bring back your love again.

Kind Summer filled our empty hearts
With love of little things,
With tiny joys of wide-eyed flowers,
And whirr of happy wings;
And Summer goes from England now,

And tired hearts and sad
With small love left are now bereft
Of everything they had.

The firelight throws upon the wall
Dream shadows as of old,
But there's no fire in all the world
Can keep our hearts from cold;
The lamps are dim behind the blind
That once shone bravely bright,
And love alone by the hearthstone
Keeps watch and ward tonight.

Dead roses lie beneath the wall
As Youth lies at the ages' feet,
The leaping shadows flicker low,
The newsboy calls along the street;
O dear days crying, dead dreams sighing,
Hush you of your pain,
For all your tears the barren years
Will not bring back your love again,
Can never bring your love again.

Since They Have Died

Since they have died to give us
gentleness,
And hearts kind with contentment

and quiet mirth,
Let us who live give also happiness
And love, that's born of pity, to the
earth.

For, I have thought, some day they may
lie sleeping
Forgetting all the weariness and pain,
And smile to think their world is in our
keeping,
And laughter come back to the earth
again.

Love 1916

One said to me, 'Seek Love, for he is Joy
Called by another name'.
A Second said, 'Seek Love, for he is
Power
Which is called Fame'.
Last said a Third, 'Seek Love, his name is
Peace'.
I called him thrice,
And answer came, 'Love now
Is christened Sacrifice'.

In November 1916 Bevil was heavily engaged
at the battle of Ancre:

We have been shooting hard since 5.45am and the battle has been raging in the densest of fogs.

Meanwhile May continued to work long hours at Oxford University Press and wrote:

Mercifully we were all used to books, indexes, typewriters and files. I remember the evening light coming in through the long windows and proofs coming up from somewhere called 'downstairs', and the smell of printers' ink and writing 'herewith please find revised and old proofs' to go off in a packet to some learned person; and a lot of people coming in to see my Father in the tower about *Why We Are at War?* which was being written then; and later going home through Little Clarendon Street and St Giles with the news boys calling the latest from the Front — British in Retreat 'orrible slaughter.

Evening

The office fire burns low, the Autumn wind
Beats suddenly against the window-pane,

The low bowed heads bend closer to the
page:
Turn up the lights, the days draw in
again.

The door swings to and shuts, the
workers wake
To evening and the end of throbbing
day;
A paper boy goes shouting down the
street —
What news of England, half the world
away?

Put on the stamps, nor storm nor
German hate
Shall cause one English keel to lose the
tide;
The streets are shadow dark, what news
tonight
Of England out by Hooge and Yser side?

For gain or loss the post goes on its
way,
The stars shine pitiful; beneath the light
Of blurred street lamps the telegrams are
read —
Good news, and so, good dreams to you
tonight.

Bevil wrote home on 2nd December 1916:

We have come out to rest and have just arrived in our final billet. Our village is well built and very straggly with low hills behind us and the marshy meadows in front; through the meadows flows a tributary of the Somme which joins that river near Abbeville. Our Mess looks on the gun park and the horse lines are in a nice meadow. Here I have been interrupted by the biggest rag since Oxford; a thing I have longed to see — a local fire — especially as it was not in any one of our billets. It was in a large barn next door to the Mess of another Battery. The Brigade orderly ran in with the news. I called the men out with every available bucket and we arrived to find the large barn full of straw alight from end to end. The barn joined two small farms. The people removed the furniture. First of all we cut the two farms off from the barn with axes — this is only possible with French houses — Then, with the two chains of buckets, we watered both ends of the barn and had it well in hand when the local fire brigade arrived from a village about two miles away, amid screams from the crowd . . . But the fire brigade were three men in different shapes of beautifully polished helmets! The hose and pump would not work for 20 minutes and ten Frenchmen on each length of hosepipe were trying very forcibly to prove that they were wrongly coupled together. When the first gush of water came they bagged the Colonel; a little later the chief fireman directing the hose in his efforts to get away from a falling beam tripped and fell into the farm midden. All the Frenchmen shouting and waving their arms the whole time and the chains of buckets interrupted at times because every Artilleryman was too weak from laughing . . . Another fire engine arrived but the pump wouldn't work. The straw in the barn continues to smoulder but all the local firemen are now blotto, insensible and the farmers are opening casks of wine to celebrate the great evening.

1917

Tight traces on the Trinity Gun (by courtesy of Trinity College, Oxford)

Bevil wrote home on 22 March 1917:

I have been really having a great time. The morning I came up from the Wagon Line to the Battery, patrols had reported the enemy's front trenches empty and he was shelling villages and roads behind his lines. I promptly ordered the horses up and by 3pm was crossing our trenches with one section. Movement was slow to start with, as trenches had to be bridged and the going was very bad. However, once over the worst part, we went roaming all over the country and had a glorious time coming into action and firing a few rounds at machine guns in copses, then a few rounds at enemy's cavalry. Meanwhile the remainder of the Battery came on more steadily and the transport had an awful time in shell holes. The water cart filled itself over the top and the Mess cart came in two and such like jokes. I spent nights curled up in my mackintosh in a ruin or behind a hedge . . . We came out today with the Division for rest . . . The Bosche had destroyed everything and even cut down the trees in orchards and every house and cellar had been blown up or pulled across the road by tractors with a wire hawser.

May noted in her autobiography:

I think 1917 was the worst year of the war for civilians. The Somme had depressed everyone and it was a cold, long winter and we were tired. Food became really difficult. There was a shortage of potatoes and people stood in the rain in long queues hoping for an odd pound . . . The new Ministry of Food issued a scheme of voluntary rationing. It was nerve racking because one felt one might be taking more than one's share and said, 'No thank you,' or if one said, 'Yes please,' ate nervously which did no good.

May wrote about her first volume of poems in her autobiography and describes how she got them published:

That spring I collected such verse as I thought 'possible,' got my Father to 'cast an eye over it,' and set forth to see Mr Blackwell. He had a small office up an uncarpeted stair at the back of the famous bookshop in the Broad. At the last moment my Father said he would come with me. I think that he wanted to make sure that I was not published in any series or involved in any clique.

On the Line of March by Captain Gilbert Holiday, RFA

Mr Blackwell was, I remember, very kind, but as I was practically blind and deaf with nerves I have a blurred recollection of what happened. My Father and I walked up the Broad together afterwards and suddenly realising that his ridiculous daughter was struggling with tears, he stopped dead. 'Why are you crying?' 'I'm not,' I said, using the old formula; 'It's all right only I did think he might take it.'

'But he has!' 'Has he?' I asked astounded. 'Yes, of course,' said my Father, continuing up the street; 'The trouble with you and that young man is that you have both got the Oxford Manner so badly you can't understand each other.' He seemed amused. As I have never been able to discover what the Oxford Manner is, I have never known what he meant.

In War Time was published by B H Blackwell in 1917.

May sent Bevil a copy and he replied from the Front on June 21st 1917:

If a heathen can be grateful for a work of art, I feel he must write and thank you for the pleasure it gave to read those poems.

Out here I have read more books than during the rest of my life, not perhaps saying much, among the books have been several War Novels and War Poems which naturally collect in a Battery Library, but there is only one which brings the war home in a unique and beautiful way.

Bevil then goes on to tell May a little about life at the Front with the horses:

Here with the Royal 9th we are cheerful and at present in a peaceful part of the line. I went on leave when things had quietened down and came back to find that Horse Shows and Sports were to form half of our daily work and a far more strenuous half than fighting the wily Bosche. We won five firsts at the Brigade Show and I began to turn my energies to turning out a really good Artillery team in really good harness in a really good wagon so we painted and burnished and groomed and at the Divisional Show we were 2nd which was disappointing as we had really attempted too much in too short a time. However two teams were sent to the Corps Show and there we were 1st easily, avenging our defeat, because the teams that beat us before, were not placed. We are now

The Corps Horse Show and Bevil's Artillery Team *(by courtesy of Trinity College, Oxford)*

making improvements for the Army Show. For the Battery the Turn-out is the chief event but we also won a 1st at Division and 2nd at Corps for the best pair of horses and, two 2nds for a single horse, 2nd for jumping and 1st for Tug-of-War. If I visit many more shows I shall feel like a person at Smithfield who prods the fat beasts and can tell their weight at a glance ... It is very funny trying to lead a double life [sic] of farmer, horse dealer and sailor. How many people at the Horse Show would imagine me taking in a reef off St Albans or really happy anchored fishing off Scilly and then picture Grose [a family friend] watching me transformed into riding breeches and training the Royal 9th winning team. I hope I shall not become a half and half and spend my dotage in a blue jersey and field boots. Best wishes to all at Magdalen Gate House.

Spring 1917

Lift up your hearts! Lord, we have lifted them
Above the tumult and the tears of War

To the dear promise of Thy Christmas
star,
We lift them up, but Thou art very far.

Lift up your hearts! O Lord, who for our
need
Givest again the promise of Thy Spring,
Grant a small hope to light our
travelling,
And for our hearts to love some little
thing.

May wrote:

I was lucky for after the Somme there was a
change of heart among poets. Siegfried
Sassoon wrote to the Press from France
saying that the war was now a war of
conquest and without justification, and
declared himself to be a conscientious
objector. He was rescued from trouble by
Robert Graves and his friends who claimed
a breakdown. C E Montague wrote *Dis-
enchantment* and Wilfred Owen was much
influenced by him. A saying went round,
'Went to the war with Rupert Brooke and
came home with Siegfried Sassoon.' I had
much admired some of Sassoon's verse but
I was not coming home with him. Someone
must go on writing for those who were still

convinced of the right of the cause for which they had taken up arms.

May's attitudes were very different from other First World War poets of the time. She continued to believe fervently in the righteousness of war even after 1916. Sassoon had attacked women's ignorance of war's real nature in 'Glory of Women':

You make us shells. You listen with delight,
By tales of dirt, and danger fondly thrilled.
You crown our distant ardours while we
fight,
And mourn our laurelled memories
when we're killed.

It was for this reason that May had little empathy for Siegfried Sassoon.

Bevil wrote the following Alphabet and sent it to May:

A   is our Army, which with impunity
    Bill said he'd smash at his first
    opportunity.

B   is the Base which is called St Nazaire,
    No longer the home of the gallant and
    fair.

C   is the charge of the Scottish of London.
    From the papers you'd argue they only
    had done one.

D   is De Wet who thought it was wiser
    to break his allegiance and follow the
    Kaiser.

E   is the End of this horrible war
    it will probably last for a century more.

F   is the Flares which never seem lacking,
    sent up by the Germans to see who's
    attacking.

G   are the Germans, a race much maligned,
    A more peace loving people you hardly
    could find.

H   are the Huns, their nearest of kin.
    A pastoral people, they are said to have
    been.

I   am the writer, a perfect nonentity;
    that is the reason I hide my identity.

J   is the Joy on the faces of men
    when they are told they must go down for
    rations at ten.

K   is the Kaiser, who is said to be balmy;
    we always feel safe when he's leading his
    army.

L   is the Lake that protects us from fire.
    They call it a trench when the weather is
    drier.

M   stands for Mud, to describe which foul
    stuff
    violent blasphemy's hardly enough.

N   is the Noise which we generally hear
    on the night when the Germans are
    issued with beer.

O   is the Order obeyed with a yawn —
    'Stand to your arms,' it's an hour till
    dawn.

P   is the Post which generally brings
    parcels of perfectly valueless things.

Q   is the Question we all do abhor
    concerning the probable end to the war.

R   stands for R-hum and also for Russian,
    our two greatest allies when fighting the
    Prussian.

S   as you know always stands for Supplies
    whose excellent qualities no one denies.

T   is Tobacco that beautiful stuff
    and thanks be to Heaven we've now got
    enough.

U   stands for Unlan who's gained notoriety,
    both for his kindness and wonderful
    piety.

V   is the Voice of the turtle dove, which bird
    has been turned into stew, so it's no
    longer heard.

W   stands for Wine, Women and War;
    we'll see to the first when the latter is
    o'er.

X   is a perfectly horrible letter.
    I'll leave it alone and I couldn't do better.

Y   stands for YPRES, which the Germans
    desire.
    They shelled it as soon as they had to
    retire.

Z   stands for Zeppelins, who long to raid
    a circus, a square and a certain arcade.

May wrote in the summer of 1917:

It rained a good deal but it rained heavier
in Flanders where they were fighting the
third battle of Ypres that ended in
Passchendaele. It was the wettest August
for years and Flanders turned to mud. Men
waded in it up to their waists, fell into it off
the duckboards and drowned in it, begging
passing comrades to shoot them rather
than leave them to that dreadful death.
Bevil, wrestling with his guns and horses,
sank in the mud and sleeping, when he
could sleep, curled up in his mackintosh in
any hole he could find, worked desperately
to save his horses which he loved and 'had
to use my revolver a good deal'. In
September he was wounded again, 'Nothing to worry about only a bit of stray iron
and a cut and bruised shoulder and arm'.
He refused to go out of the line and was
furious because, contrary to his orders, he
was reported wounded in the lists.

And for later on in 1917 May recorded:

It dried up in November and on the 20th
381 massed tanks broke through the
German Line at Cambrai and reached
open country, and for the first and last time

bells were rung in London to celebrate a victory. But it was too soon. For five consecutive days it rained and on the first three there was snow and sleet. On the 19th Bevil had written home that they were moved forward but digging themselves out of the mud and he had been up all night trying to get his wagons and horses out of it. On the 29th he was more hopeful and wrote of Cambrai as a success but it did not seem much like one to us. We were in a bad way by the end of the year. Butchers' shops closed in the middle of the mornings with notices: No beef, no mutton; grocers also shut with notices: Sold out.

1918

May and Dorothea had met Bevil in London in January 1918 and seen J M Barrie's latest play, '*Dear Brutus*' together.

Bevil sent a letter to May on 3rd February:

> I was glad to know you had enjoyed the day in Town so much, you must think how I enjoyed it too ... We are very comfortable just now and things are very quiet ... and I spend a very leisurely time walking up to the Infantry Battalions and around the trenches three or four times a week. Twice a week I ride over to see the horses at the wagon line ... This all sounds very dull but I thought you might like to have some idea of life during rather dull winter warfare. The other day our aeroplanes had a combined straffe on Bosche captive balloons. They set two on fire but, when the observers saw our planes approaching, they all took to their parachutes. A long row of dangling Huns drawn out across the front looked simply priceless. Through our glasses we saw quite a crowd collect to welcome one of them as he landed on the earth. I suspect there was much Got-Straffing of England [this was a German slogan during the war

meaning God punish England]. I wonder if they enjoyed their tea after it.

On the 21st March the Germans launched the 'Great Offensive' and suddenly Bevil was busy again. The 'Great Offensive' was an all-out attack on the Western Front before the Americans had time to move in too many troops.

Bevil wrote the following in April (this is from an account called *With a Field Battery in Spring* 1918 written by Bevil Quiller-Couch, typed up by May and kept by her as a record of his time at war):

My Battery has just come out of action after eight memorable days in the centre of the great battle which started when the German High Command launched their March offensive. Two days' trek has brought us to the reserve area on the river Canche, near Faevent, where Divisions refit and rest . . . Of the old Officers in my Battery, one subaltern and myself alone have survived the past fortnight, and the gun detachments have also suffered heavily; most of the casualties being slight gas poisoning from the days of perpetual bombardment with gas shells. All of us old hands were only just recovering our voices as the result of the same frightfulness and at one time in the battle there was no one who could raise his voice above a whisper.

May wrote:

Their first attack had carried the Germans across the Battlefields of the Somme . . . Their second against the British on the 9th April, was a desperate endeavour to finish their advance as they had planned. Haig who knew that if only he could hold long enough, the reserves he needed so badly, might yet be found, held on grimly and sent his famous Dispatch — 'With our backs to the wall and believing in the justice of our cause, each one of us must fight on to the end'. That call rallied his almost exhausted troops and shook England at home. They held on and the Germans turned to the attack of the French across the Marne and came to within forty miles of Paris; but there, and in Haig's battlefield, the line remained unbroken.

In April Bevil wrote again to May:

Leave, I suppose, may be out of the question for some time, but I shall look forward with hope and am coming to see you this time ... I have rather an 'Extraordinary Story' to tell you but it is too long for a letter so I will leave it till we meet.

In July Bevil wrote again:

I hear you are off to Fowey for a few days ... I am awfully sad as I had hoped to be there too at that time ... Perhaps your visit may be put off until August when I shall get home even if I have to desert.

And to his parents he wrote:

May Cannan, I suppose, is with you now. I hope she enjoys herself. She was always my favourite and I was very sorry not to be home during part of her visit.

At the beginning of August May left for Paris. She had been accepted to work in the War Office Department in Paris. She wrote:

Generally we were known as the 'British Mission', actually we were the BCI (The Bureau Central Interallie) and a branch of

90

M15. Four girls worked in Trade which dealt with smuggling over frontiers and other duller things and five girls in Espionage.

May worked in Trade to start with but within two weeks she was transferred permanently to Espionage.

Bevil now wrote to May in Paris in August:

No leave yet . . . I shall certainly try for Paris leave, in fact I should have tried long ago if I thought my English leave was going to be so long . . . I shall be a regular country cousin so will you show me around and I will open my mouth and say the right thing with an open guide book in my right hand.

Bevil did get his English leave at the beginning of September but of course May was now in Paris.

May wrote:

On the 29th September Bevil had led his Battery into action over the hill at Noyelles. On the 16th October they were all moved forward and The End, though we still couldn't believe it was true, could be seen. On the 18th there was St Vaast and on the 20th there were rumours that the whole Belgian Coast was reported captured and the Whole Line advanced. On the 26th Bevil was wounded again and very angry because the War Office reported it — 'A small piece stuck in my hand and a cut on the elbow was the only damage I pulled the piece out'.

On 30th October Bevil wrote to May:

I shall try for some Paris leave ... Of course I shan't get it till we come out for a rest, but I hope it will come off about the second week in November ... I will try and tell you about our last battle. We moved up to positions in the wildest weather ... the battle started at 3.30 the following morning. It had stopped raining but was very foggy. By 7.30 we had completed our part of the barrage and were moving forward to a new position in a hedge by a river bank which I, riding ahead, had chosen. It cleared soon after we got there and turned out a perfect day. By 9am I had a telephone wire to the hill in front and was engaging the most glorious targets as Fritz was now very rattled and

92

blocking the roads with transports and guns, behind his lines. We were firing with very short intervals all day. During the next night it froze and it was rather bleak supporting our Infantry when they resumed the attack at 4.30 the next morning . . . Then we were moving forward again and trotted through a village where the French inhabitants were peering through their cellar gratings and cheering in a dull way being half stunned with the events of the last 24 hours. They had suffered from Bosche gas shelling during the night. We advanced a long way before coming into action again about midday. During the afternoon we had a great duel with a Bosche Field Battery until, after driving off their teams which were trying to save them, our infantry finally captured the six guns complete. Then we turned the captured Battery round on the Bosche until we had finished off all their ammunition. Here we finally settled down and have been living in a hole under a bank for three days.

Bevil wrote home on the 4th November 1918:

The Battery is in a position of readiness after supporting the initial attack at dawn this morning. It looks like a big thing;

prisoners are plentiful and several guns have been taken already. We are all anxiously awaiting orders . . . I think this will be one of the last battles of the War. Everyone out here is very pleased with the work done by the Allied Statesmen and Military advisors in Paris. It has been done quickly, cleanly and sternly and I can't help thinking that few people will be able to grumble unless the Bosche liver shrivels. Personally I don't think he will hesitate. Even before signing, every day puts him in a worse position here and if the present authorities won't sign the German people will soon put up someone who will.

On the night of 4/5th November Bevil and his battery fired their last barrage before the Armistice and went into reserve at Villers Pol. Bevil had fought his last battle.

His war was over and he knew that his Battery would not fire again. He set out for Paris on November 10th and this is how he described his trip when he next wrote home:

I left the Battery like Dick Whittington and took the road with my kit on my back . . . I made my way by lifts to Cambrai where there is an officer's club. There I put up for the night and took to the road again early after breakfast the next morning . . . the weather was beautiful. I got well on the way to Amiens and strolled off the main road to have my lunch by an old battery position on the Somme battlefield. At the control telephone box at what had once been a wayside station stood a Sapper and I went over just to pass the time of day.

Sapper: 'Going on leave, Sir?'

Bevil: 'No, making my way to Amiens.'

Sapper: 'There's an empty goods train due here in ten minutes going through Amiens, Sir.'

Bevil: 'Good.'

Sapper: 'Well Sir, it's all over at last!'

Thus I hear of the termination of the Great War. I simply could not realise it as I stood there with the strange Sapper alone in the midst of the deserted Somme battlefield.

In a few minutes, my train came and I was comfortably settled with two more Sappers who were in charge of the train . . . Again we discussed the news and I sat watching the familiar landscape pass by. I longed to be with you all and embrace you, or to be back with the Battery who are my children; to be with people that I knew to rejoice and share that wonderful feeling of joy and thankfulness. The train reached

Amiens and, as I left the station, I was seized by a whirling crowd and carried into the Square. Everywhere people were singing and dancing, cheering or crying. It was like a wonderful dream.

And the next day Bevil reached Paris and wrote:

On reaching the Gare du Nord the scene was immense. I was carried onto a chariot draped in flowers and bunting and pulled along the street with an American doctor, three Chasseurs Alpines [French light infantry] two French Artillery officers and a mixed crowd of Poilus [French private soldiers] in the car. Thus did I enter a strange city.

Meanwhile back in May's office in Paris there were other concerns. May wrote:

We watched the flags move on the big map in the Colonel's room and could not believe what we saw, and turned to our other enemies; the bitter cold and the 'flu. It was the forerunner of the great epidemic of 1919. They had it in England too and my mother wrote anxious for my Father who was tired. Paris was swept by it. There were no doctors or drugs to be had and people died like flies and the city was draped in black as they hung the curtains out over the house doors. The French War Office released rum for us . . . It hung in the air. A feeling of terrified uncertainty, almost of terrified hope.

The Armistice

In an Office in Paris

The news came through over the
telephone:
All the terms had been signed: the War
was won:
And all the fighting and the agony,
And all the labour of the years were
done.
One girl clicked sudden at her typewriter
And whispered, 'Jerry's safe', and sat and
stared:
One said, 'It's over, over, it's the end:
The War is over: ended': and a third,
'I can't remember life without the war.'
And one came in and said, 'Look here,
they say
We can all go at five to celebrate,
As long as two stay on, just for today.'

It was quite quiet in the big empty room
Among the typewriters and little piles
Of index cards: one said, 'We'd better just
Finish the day's reports and do the files.'
And said, 'It's awf'lly like *Recessional*,
Now when the tumult has all died away.'
The other said, 'Thank God we saw it through;
I wonder what they'll do at home today.'

And said, 'You know it will be quiet tonight
Up at the Front: first time in all these years,
And no one will be killed there any more,'
And stopped, to hide her tears.
She said, 'I've told you; he was killed in June.'
The other said, 'My dear, I know; I know . . .
It's over for me too . . . My man was killed,
Wounded . . . and died . . . at Ypres
. . . three years ago . . .
And he's my Man, and I want him,' she said,
And knew that peace could not give back her Dead.

May Cannan
(by courtesy of Jim Slater)

Bevil Quiller-Couch
(*by courtesy of Guy Symondson*)

May described November 11 1918 in her autobiography:

On the morning of November 11th I was called into the Colonel's room to take some notes from the telephone. They were all there and got up and made room for me at the table. A voice, very clear, thank God, said 'Ready?' and began to dictate the Terms of the Armistice. They muttered a bit, crowding round me and I said fiercely, 'Oh shut up, I can't hear' and the skies didn't fall. I wrote in my private short-long-hand and half my mind was in a prayer that I should be able to read it back. I could feel my heart thumping and hear the silence in the room round me. When the voice stopped, I said mechanically 'understood' and got up. I made four copies of what I had written and took them in and went back to my little office and told the staff. I can't remember much of what we said: I can only remember being so cold, and crying and trying not to let the others see. That night it was all over Paris. There were sounds of cheering and rejoicing down the boulevards as I walked home.

Paris, November 11, 1918

Down on the boulevards the crowds went by,
The shouting and the singing died away,
And in the quiet we rose to drink the toasts,
Our hearts uplifted to the hour, the Day:
The King — the Army — Navy — the Allies —
England — and Victory.
And then you turned to me and with low voice
(the tables were abuzz with revelry),
'I have a toast for you and me', you said,
And whispered 'Absent', and we drank
Our unforgotten Dead.
But I saw Love go lonely down the years,
And when I drank, the wine was salt
with tears.

For A Girl

Go cheering down the boulevards
And shout and wave your flags,
Go dancing down the boulevards

In all your gladdest rags:
And raise our cheers and wave your flags
And kiss the passer-by,
But let me break my heart in peace
For all the best men die.
    It was 'When the War is over
    Our dreams will all come true,
    When the War is over
    I'll come back to you';
    And the War is over, over,
    And they never can come true.

Go cheering down the boulevards
In all your brave array,
Go singing down the boulevards
To celebrate the day:
But for God's sake let me stay at home
And break my heart and cry,
I've loved and worked, and I'll be glad,
But all the best men die.
    It was 'When the War is over
    Our dreams will all come true,
    When the War is over
    I'll come back to you';
    And the War is over, over,
    And they never can come true.

Bevil had arrived in Paris on the 12th
November. On the 13th he went straight to
May's office, which he had warned he might

do: 'I shall put in for Paris leave as soon as this is over and just blow into your office.'

May wrote:

> I was quite unprepared when it came. I was clearing up before going back to lunch when Captain V put his head into my office and said, 'Oh, Miss Cannan, there's a Major Quiller-Couch asking for you downstairs. Would you go?' He was standing in the hall. In rather faded Khaki and a Field Gunner's leggings and boots, looking up, his hat in his hand. And suddenly, blindingly and convincingly and against all reason, I knew why he had come. The place went dark about me and a darkness roared in my ears. I clutched the banister rail to prevent myself pitching down those stairs, and went slowly down, the darkness clearing as I went. Slowly and irrevocably and against all reason, I went down to meet him.

Bevil and May had five days together. Bevil sent a line home but, for the moment, kept his secret:

> I am having a wonderful time here . . . No doubt *The Times* will be reporting some of

the great doings in this Capital. After seeing a little of the procession and the preliminary scenes, May and I went out to St Cloud and had a very simple lunch by the river. Afterwards we went for a long walk in the Bois Meudon. In the evening we dined at a most cheerful place in the Boulevard Italien and we had a table by the window and watched the wild scenes of rejoicing in the streets. On the way home we had to take part in the rejoicings. We danced in circles, were smothered in confetti and were embraced by excited men and women. I hope Mr and Mrs Cannan would not have thought it very terrible.

And May wrote:

We went to Versailles and walked by the pink pillars of the Petits Trianons and dined very quietly together in the Rue St Honore with two very grand Generals who obviously wondered what a much deco-rated Gunner Major and a tired looking girl in a black frock were doing there that night. And the next day, he fetched me from the office at 1pm and we walked down to the Pont d'Alma, and there, looking down into the waters of the Seine, hurrying by and having known other wars

and other lovers, he asked me to marry
him.

Paris Leave

Do you remember, in Paris, how we two
dined
On your Leave's last night,
And the happy people around us who
laughed and sang,
And the great blaze of light.

And the big bow-window over the
boulevard
Where our table stood,
And the old French waitress who patted
your shoulder and
Told us that love was good.

(We had lingered so long watching the
crowds that moved
In the street below,
And saying the swift dear things of
Lovers newly met,
That she had guessed us so.)

I remember her smile, and the ring of
your spurs

On the polished stair;
And the touch of your hand, and the
clear November night,
And the flags everywhere.

I remember the Concorde, and the
fountains' splash,
The black captured guns;
And the grey-haired men with their
wives who wept and kissed, and
The lovers of their sons.

And the French girls with their poilus
who linked their hands
To dance round us two,
And sang 'Ne passeront pas,' till one
broke loose and flung
Her arms wide and kissed you.

She was all France that night, and you
brave Angleterre,
The unfailing friend;
And I cried, 'Vive la France,' and we told
each other again
The War was at an end.

It was so hard to believe it was really
won,
And the waiting past;
That the years wherein we knew death

were under our feet,
And our Love crowned at last . . .

I remember most now the faces of the girls,
And the still, clear stars.
We said we were glad later lovers would never know
The bitterness of wars.

The lamp of the courtyard gate was bright on the old
Ribbons on your breast;
And the songs and the voices died down the boulevards.
You said that Love was best.

May wrote:

And then I went back with him to the Rue Turbigo and in that strange high-ceilinged room in the Paris-France Hotel, that had suddenly become a home, sat on his bed and darned some socks and sewed on a button. He had washed a shirt and hung it to dry on a piece of string stretched across the room; and we did not know that that was to be our only housekeeping.

On their last morning together May recorded:

> I caught an early train on the Metro and we breakfasted together at the Rue Turbigo and then I walked with him to the Gare du Nord, he carrying his pack. I was wearing his ring and as the train pulled out he put his dark head down on my hands that were on the carriage window and kissed them. The train pulled out. When I could see and hear again, I found the entrance to the Metro and caught a train and went round to work.

It was at this time that Bevil told May he had asked, before sailing for France in 1914, for a few hours' leave to come to Oxford to ask her to marry him. Unfortunately that leave was not granted. Bevil wrote to May's parents at once for permission to marry May and as soon as he received it, he wrote home to his father:

> I have been bursting to write before and I hope you won't think me wrong to have held back the greatest news in the world. May has consented to marry me some day. It was by no means suddenly arranged on my part and in fact dates back some time before the War and the thought has helped

no end in carrying me through these four years, but I made a vow, May thinks wrongly, that if my family had to suffer because I was out here it was right that no more should, and it was surely right to avoid it? I also felt that it would help me to go straight from the start and not think of getting home or soft jobs, and God knows it has helped. When the Armistice seemed certain I pushed for the Paris leave and there delivered my bombshell. I have never known that life could be so great until those days but I had to wait until I heard from Mr and Mrs Cannan before I wrote to you. Their answers were perfectly charming when they came today and now I can at last unburden my mind. I know one thing — you all love May and will know that I am luckier than I deserve ... I was perhaps more in luck in the whole fall of events than any man ought to be. I trust the start gives indication of the future. Great things are settled at Versailles!

And to his mother and Foy, his sister, he wrote:

I have been longing to write for more than a fortnight to tell you that May has promised to marry me. I should have liked to have gone to see Mr and Mrs Cannan at once but as that could not be, I had to keep the secret until I heard from them today. Their answers were too great for words! This may be a bombshell, but to me it has been the greatest and one ideal which has helped to carry me through these last four years. It has been tested and proved a thousand times. Well, there came the reward of these last two months, the chance of an immediate Armistice. I could keep the secret no more and joy of joys the reason for doing so disappeared. Paris leave and the greatest thing of all. I am so happy that you all know and love May.

Q wrote to May:

That you have made me happy, happier than, I daresay, you can guess . . . If it had been any one in the world but you, indeed, I shouldn't be feeling like this nor (I think) would his Mother or Foy. So that's that and whenever you come, it'll be to take possession of a room we've all without knowing it, been preparing for you and only for you.

An' thou shall marry a proud gunner,
An' a proud gunner I'm sure he'll be.

Bless you.

and to Bevil on the subject of his
engagement:

My dearest Boy,

You will have heard by this time from your
mother and the Babe [Foy's nickname]:
both of whom seem to have been a great
deal more surprised than I was by your
announcement. But then although I never
attended it, even to myself, some sort of
little hope that this might be, was always
alive somehow at the bottom of my heart.
If ever I got round to shaping it, I promptly
suppressed it under half a dozen very wise
reflections — as that sons don't marry to
please their parents: that it would be a poor
job if they did: that no sign had ever come
to me of this being likely to happen etc. But
suppress it as I might it was there all the
while and when you wrote about the time
you and May were having in Paris and you
getting away quietly to Meudon — well,
you see, I happen to know the symptoms
and in these matters keep pretty young for

my age I thank the Lord. You know or guess how I feel and have always felt about Cannan. He has been the first of my friends from the moment we met. Then he goes and marries one of the best — and of the children, if I had a favourite one . . . but that's not worth saying. But I have taken note of her and admired her always. She has an extremely sensitive and very noble mind of which it will be your dearest privilege to be very careful. So many men, after they are married, forget that a lover should be a lover always and show it. But that is an exercise which sweetens the whole of life.

And so May now understood the 'Extraordinary Story' which was that Bevil had loved her all through the War and been intending to marry her but had not allowed himself to show it.

Bevil thought that he had saved May the anxiety of waiting for him to come home from war but May felt deprived; she felt that he had deprived her of the precious right to be anxious. 'Going alone to war,' she said, 'he had left me lonely in mine. There had been leaves and we had not shared them; letters but not for me . . . Could he not have thought that I might be, not a weakness, but a strength?' The following poem puts May's feelings into words:

The Menin Road

When you went up and down the Road,
The Menin Road, in the Great War,
I wonder if you ever thought
Of me, that was so very far.

And when you lay on windy nights
And watched the clouds blot out the
    blue,
I wonder if you thought at all
Of the dear things that we should do.

Oh, I remember it was spring
And you went riding in a wood,
Did violets blow then, in the days
Before I understood?

And it was summer once, at Mons,
Hot nights of August panting still,
And you were tired beyond all thought,
And there was nothing left, but will.

I'll never know the things you thought,
Nor half the things you used to say,

Only, you were at Ypres — and Loos —
And fought there, upon such a day.

But somehow it's on Winter nights
I see you take the Road again,
When all the earth was bursting shell,
And all the sky was pelting rain.

I used to lie awake and think,
And think, about the Old Front Line,
But that was long ago, and I
Had no right then to call you mine.

And I'll be very glad, My Dear,
When your strong hands hold mine once
more,
But oh, my heart is sad because
I never rode with you to war.

Since Were Beloved of You

Since were beloved of you
Not the Laughter alone,
But the Dream and the Tears,
Since you rode not wholly alone
The difficult years:
These for you are alone,
And the Joy, and the Tears.

Since to us both in France,
Most royally alone,
Came the Dream and the Days,
Since I go not wholly alone
The difficult ways:
These for you are alone,
And the Love and the Days.

Q said of this poem: '*Since Were Beloved of You* is a beautiful thing (but it is wicked of you to make me cry).'

After his Paris leave, Bevil rejoined his Battery that was based with the whole of the 2nd Division in Mauberge and prepared to march with them into Germany. Bevil wrote to May almost every day and his letters give a remarkable account of that final triumphant march into Germany. As the days went by he longed to be with May and his impatience to be demobilised comes through very clearly. Here are some extracts from his letters.

(20th November 1918) The march is to be done in easy stages and we are to look 'models' of the British Army which overthrew and smote the Hun so everything is to be varnished and shining, everything shabby is being changed and discarded, and the Infantry Battalions will march in full bands. It will be a wonderful experience. As yet I have not talked to any of the great ones who know, but I gather that there is no reason to think that we shall stay on in Germany long after Peace is signed . . . but when we arrive in England I shall have finished my share in the Great War and can hand in my gun. When I told the children [the men in his Battery] of my great time in Paris they were full of joy.

(24th November) Mauberge is a pretty place and the streets are thronged all day with prisoners of war of every nation. Italians, Portuguese, French, Black Troops — Americans even — and English Civilians too; all dribbling back from the enemy's camps. He seems to have opened the doors and let them wander out how and where they like, and of course the feeding and sheltering of them on their journey takes much organisation. It is very pathetic meeting some of the civilians trudging back to their old homes in the Somme area, not having heard what a wilderness there is where their village once stood.

(25th November) We marched this morning when the roads were hard with hoar frost and it was beautifully still and clear and perfect for the march . . . We are passing through civilisation again; When we got into billets about midday and had groomed and fed the horses, I rode out with the four veterans who were with this Battery when they first came into action on 24th August 1914 and we found the position and the grave of a Corporal who was killed there; beautifully kept by the civilians and planted with flowers and we solemnly planted a new wooden cross with his name painted on it. The Battery wheeler had been carefully preparing it for the past two days when I had told them that we should be marching close by.

(27th November) We are at Charleroi now on the southern edge of the great Belgium coalfields . . . We walked about 18 miles and had just a piece of cheese and biscuits . . . We shall be marching through the Ardennes for seven days, all wooded hills and deep gorges and the scenery should be priceless. You told me to write if I wanted anything. Could you send me some soap . . . We are now going, definitely, to Cologne and should reach there soon after the middle of December.

I heard rather a sweet story from a friend of mine, one Knox-Gore, now a

Lieutenant Colonel who came out as a platoon commander in this 2nd Division with the 60th Rifles in 1914. About the first day of that great retreat he left his sword with an old lady in a little French farm close to Landrecies as it was a boiling afternoon and the sword was a useless encumbrance. Since then this man was wounded as a Captain and sent out to East Africa as a Major, and finally became chief of Staff to General Nortney and came home with him this summer and was sent out to this Division for attachment to learn more about the war in France. He watched the Bosche retiring and suddenly thought he would go back and look for his sword. He found the Farm destroyed but ran across the old lady who recognised him at once and led him to another farm about a mile away owned by her son-in-law. There she conducted him up to a loft, the floor some feet deep in hay and littered with odds and ends of German equipment for the Bosche had only left a bare 24 hours before. The old lady collected her son-in-law and the two cleared away a space of flooring, levered up the floor and there, between the boards, lay the sword all wrapped up in straw and still shining when it was uncovered. Some day, May, you must write a poem about that sword.

May responded to Bevil's request by writing the following poem:

The Ballad of the Sword

The sun was hot on the Belgian plain;
They had halted and must to the road again;
He must march lighter, and that was plain.

The old farm wife by the farm gate stood,
He looked at her face, and guessed her good,
And spoke the slow French she understood.

'A sword is no sword today to fight,
We retreat for a day and a night,
I leave it with you, that will be all right?'

She looked to the South where the great road led,
She looked at the boy, and bowed her head,

120

'I will keep it till you come back,' she said.

'May the good God keep you,' she said, 'from harm;'
He dropped on the Aisne with a shattered arm,
And the war went on, and they burnt her farm.

Time and tide, and a wandering star
Brought him back from fields afar
A Colonel of Staff to end his war.

The leaves were drifted red on the plain
When he rode up the great white road again;
He sought for the farm, and sought in vain.

'There's more than any sword that's gone,' he said,
And thought of the woman and thought her dead,
And sighed and turned his horse's head.

The shadows were long, the day was spent,
He passed a woman whose back was bent

By the load she bore, and the way she
went.

He stopped on the road to speak good
day;
'There was a farm once, stood this
way,'
She answered, 'The fields stand bare
today.'

She laid a hand on his bridal arm,
'I was the woman who owned that
farm,
And, the good God kept you safe from
harm!'

She said, 'I have kept it, you shall see,
You passed the farm by the fallen tree?
'Tis my daughter's home now; come
with me.'

Her daughter came from the brown
homestead,
And led the way to the great farm shed
Hay-filled, where the soldiers had made
their bed.

She said, 'They slept here yesternight,
We guessed your coming who watched
their flight,

And we buried the sword; you will find it
bright.'

They ripped up the boards and pulled
the hay
From the hidden nest where the great
sword lay,
And the sunset struck it, a silver ray.

Not by the victory
Nor yet by Death,
Is the End attained,
The sword saith,
But by the Oldest Things
That still are true,
The smallest of the thing
That he may do;

Stronger than all strong things
The faith ye keep
Shall grow and shall abide
When he shall sleep.

Bevil wrote:

(30th November) We had a very long
march yesterday and are now only a day
off Namur and five days from Germany
... After Namur we are going to follow
the road along the banks of the Meuse

... and my children [the Battery] are very concerned that they have not got a six horse team of greys. They insist that an Officers' Team should turn out at our wedding and an ammunition wagon with bottles and flowers shall gallop in the rear. I am afraid that the 9th Battery will probably be much changed before it comes home as a Battery. The schemes for demobilisation sound so business-like I have visions of all my miners and schoolmasters being taken away quite soon ... I hope to God there is a mail today though I don't let the children notice it but when one comes ... I always told them it was maddening if a man who was engaged, sat staring into the fire for hours.

May wrote in her autobiography:

On the 3rd of December I said farewell to a rather sad office and on the night of 4/5th crossed a very stormy sea and came into Southampton water. It had been a nightmare journey, with a taxi that failed to arrive, trains that ran late, drunks on the trams at Havre, and midnight darkness on the docks where I stumbled through pools of water to my ship, and I was deadly tired.

As the train pulled into Oxford I took off my gloves feeling for my ring and wondering a little what had befallen me, so came home.

Bevil wrote:

(5th December) I am now in better spirits than ever, having had your letter ... I have just written to Charles Cannan Esq ... I loved his first letter and felt it was just right. In fact I had expected a letter of one sentence, 'Dear Bevil, you must give me time to think of such sudden announcements' — I hope he did not think I was a wild young man who might run away with you ... I must tell you about our wanderings ... We left Presles early yesterday and marched in sun and wind to the outskirts of Namur — Malonne was the actual village on the South Bank of the Sambre. There we had all our horses in a Tannery and we all lived in a big public school. Our Mess was the Senior Common Room and the old Dons (Monks of course) came and talked to us in their best English and compared the place to Eton ... Unfortunately we have no Etonians or else we might have made them rather heated. The people were very kind and we had hare for dinner . . . Today we were off again at 9.30 . . . We marched along for eight miles and are now billeted in a place called Namêche on the river bank. After stables, I borrowed a boat and took Marshall for a long row and we called on Brigade Headquarters by boat . . . Tomorrow the march continues. We cross over here to the opposite bank and continue by the river all day, a 14-mile march to Huy. There are tugs and barges and heaps of things that appeal to me.

(6th December) Today we continued along the Meuse. When we came to Huy, where we are now billeted, it was just as good as ever and the town very pretty . . . You are a dear to remember about Handley Cross. I shall simply love it and I shall read it to Funny Face. He used to be a wonderful hunter in his young days and in spite of his 20 years his legs are as clean as a whistle . . . Charles Cannan tells me *The Times* should make an announcement soon . . . You must let me know when I have to put up the flags . . . The children are pulling my leg because I do so much letter writing and get such large mails . . . When you write your book for me it won't be sad, will it? Could you write '*My March to Germany*'?

(8th December) We were in Huy when I finished my last letter, billeted in a huge Chateau looking on the Meuse ... The next day we marched south away from the Meuse and up a little valley. Then up an enormous hill and along a country of scattered farms and pine woods with occasional little villages. We billeted in one of these — Warzée — last night and started again this morning. Very soon we struck the most gorgeous scenery as we descended into the valley of the Ourthe and followed the river to Comblain-La-Tour. Then up another enormous two mile hill and along high wooded country to the village of Harzé, which is in a hollow on a little stream running into the River Ambleve. We strike this river tomorrow and follow it until we come near Malmédy where we will turn lefthanded and cross the Frontier ... I have walked nearly all the way so I feel as strong as a lion.

Bevil and May's engagement was announced formally in *The Times* on 11th December.

MAJOR B B QUILLER-COUCH
AND MISS CANNAN

The engagement is announced of Major Bevil B Quiller-Couch MC, RFA only son of Sir Arthur and Lady Quiller-Couch, The Haven, Fowey to May Wedderburn Cannan, second daughter of Mr and Mrs Cannan, Magdalen Gate House, Oxford.

Bevil continued to write to May:

(12th December) I am writing from Elsenborn Barracks where we are all comfortably settled, where the Old Hun used to swagger up and down Hock Hocking to der tag, but now so mean and humble! Yesterday we crossed the frontier and the Royal 9th all waved their hats and cheered. It was a ripping march all along the Ambleve valley and we billeted in Malmédy, a very jolly town . . . the only gripe I have about getting into Germany is the sudden change from flags and decorations and joyful faces but the people are tame enough and all out to be polite and behave. At the very frontier there were two inns, one Belgian all decorated with flags and holly and fir, the other ten yards away from it, gloomy and sullen. Today we left the glorious hill country for rather dull fields and farms.

(13ᵗʰ December) We marched along the muddy road getting wetter and wetter. Towards the end of the march the country was simply perfect . . . the billet is most awfully palatial, owned by a young Bosche officer who was invalided out of their army owing to wounds early in the War, and he has given us all the best rooms and is very polite . . . Now the great joy — the mail — our families are dears. It was a great surprise to them. Mother was most awfully pleased . . . Foy writes that the news has made Mother like a two-year-old. We have always agreed in the people we are fond of — Aunt Jane is longing to know you — she adds Betty always hoped it would be May (renewed cheers). Even Mr Phelps of Fowey (the boatman) has written as Mother had to tell him! I shall keep all the letters for you to see . . . Your letters from Paris arrived by the same post so I feel I could do anything . . . Isn't it wonderful . . . I am so glad we finished the war in Paris . . . for the French, after the English, are a great people and deserve to have a share in our happiness.

(16ᵗʰ December) I have thought of you as 'Dearest May' for such a long time. Our march has not finished yet. We have passed through Elesenborn and Kesternich and are now just out of the hill country and down on the broad valley of the Rhine near Düren.

(20ᵗʰ December) We marched to our final home for the next few weeks today — Langerwehe — a topping little town tucked in a little valley at the foot of the Hills. Really it is easily the best place for Artillery we have ever been to and the Battery has the whole village to itself.

(23ʳᵈ December) Do you think we could get married soon after I am demobilised and we could have a great honeymoon and holiday in one and then go back with sleeves rolled up for the great beginning in the garret?

(25ᵗʰ December) After a succession of gales we had a perfect day yesterday and I rode into Düren on Funny Face . . . I have a lot to do with the housekeeping of the whole

Battery . . . I am shortly to take violent exercise carving the Men's Christmas dinner . . . I hope someone will produce a Christmas mail and a letter from you . . . I tried to picture our Christmas next year.

(27th December) Well, our Christmas was a glorious success and we wound up with carols sung by the cooks, and crackers and carols sung by the Officers . . . tomorrow we are having a variety evening with songs, boxing in the gymnasium . . . then we are going to organise hockey, rugger, running and indoor games.

(30th December) I have told them that I must get leave as soon as possible because you have such a lot to tell me and because my previous employers want to talk business with me . . . I would like to fix up plans during the leave and ask you if you think you could marry me as soon after I am demobilised as possible . . . I love your letters and am more happy every time another arrives.

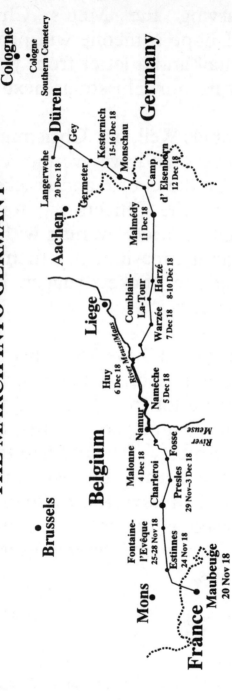

This map shows the route the 9th Battery, Royal Field Artillery took on their advance into Germany in Nov/Dec 1918 commanded by Major BB Quiller-Couch DSO, MC.

EARLY 1919

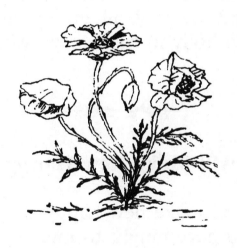

Bevil wrote:

(1st January) One of my best army friends a Major Haining who started the great war with Couch, has written his congratulations from Aldershot where he is now lecturing ... The Hainings are a topping pair ... Father says he and Mother drink our health often and look forward to decorating for us another Christmas and May shall help decorate the tree. Couch will also assist and we will all go up in the boat gathering holly in the Lerryn woods.

Now I will Make New Happy Songs

Now I will make new happy songs
That you have taught to me,
Of windy nights in Paris town,
Of stars in Picardy;
But best of all when Summer comes,
My Dear, for you and me.

Now I will make new happy songs
That you have taught to me,
Of English roses born in June,
Of dreams in Picardy;

But best of all in early June,
My Dear, for you and me.

Now I will make new happy songs,
For you will come to me
Safe with the sunlight on your sword
From fields of Picardy,
To go with me, My Dear, and teach
The song of songs to me.

May wrote:

On the 1st of January Bevil had written,
'This will be a wonderful year — Our year
— *Annus Mirabilis*' — and it did so begin.

And Bevil continued to write to May:

(2nd January 1919) I had three letters from
you yesterday . . . I am so glad you want
me to wear uniform at the wedding and
Fergus Graham will be best man please
. . . He is my first man friend . . . and he is
awfully bucked about it. He says it puts the
Armistice quite in the shade . . . I am so
happy that you enjoyed your Christmas too
and we were both surrounded by cheerful
people. Funny Face is calling me and he
looks younger every day and has come to
take me to visit a Howitzer Battery.

(4ᵗʰ January) Yesterday I spent wrestling with demobilisation . . . It is a gigantic job . . . The only thing that annoys me is the continual wail which goes up about the shortage of rolling stock and our long communications which make supplies and letters so long and all the time the Fat Hun is allowed to keep a much better local service than you have between Reading and London, or between the most important places in England. Here at the village station you can get a civilian train in either direction nearly every hour . . . You must educate me in poetry — I am appallingly ignorant and the only thing that can be said for my ignorance is that there are great things for the future. A few of Kipling's poems, William Shakespeare, M W Cannan and half a dozen other poems are literally the only ones I have ever read.

(5ᵗʰ January) I am going to Cologne tomorrow in order to be able to report on that City and bring some of its scented water home to the Independent Young Lady when I come . . . I had long letters from home and they are all longing to see us and Foy says heaps of people have been demanding to see your photo.

(7th January) Yesterday Marshall and I had a splendid day in Cologne ... we came back by train with 17 in a carriage, French, German and English and I did the *Pater Familias* and looked after a sweet child aged seven; and although she could only talk Bosche we managed to make each other understood and we struck up a great friendship and when we got out her mother curtsied and gave me a blessing ... Afterwards the Burgomaster [sic] came to see me on important business and I had two civilians in our lock up who had been caught out after dark without a pass. This morning I sat as JP of Langerwehe and administered justice. Then I had to survey the railway line in this area and make arrangements for a grand inspection of the Brigade by the Corps Commander.

(8th January) Our inspection today was a great success and the Corps Commander who was inclined to be peevish at first was hardly allowed to get a word in. I rushed him round so fast that his staff panted behind ... and he told me to congratulate all ranks and that he was especially pleased with the condition of the horses; and as he didn't know a horse from a mule I was much amused ... Afterwards I sat as JP and fined two Bosche £1.00 each or seven day's imprisonment and their wives were waiting outside and came and laid their £1s before me and curtsied. Oh Potentate! ... Peggy [Bevil's horse] is in splendid form and she loves us.

Bevil took his two weeks English leave from 13th – 27th January, crossing over from Germany and arriving in Oxford to be with May. They travelled down to Fowey — at last together. On the train May wrote the following poem.

The Ballad of the Independent Young Woman

When you come home with the Battery
Come home from the Great War
When you come home with the Battery
And ride to France no more;
When the great bees dream of clover
And roses are red in June,
And the war is over, over,
We'll have our honeymoon.

You came to teach what I couldn't learn
Hot from the battle
When you come home with no 'return',
On the old Cologne express,
I'll climb down from my office stool
Where I need to sit so high,
And to paper and pencil and pen and
ruler
I'll say a long goodbye.

I went about this wonderful world
With an independent mean
And flew the flag that I'd never furled
Since I was seventeen,
Till you came over to Paris town
A gunner with guns to lay,
And battered my castle defences down
And carried my flag away.

We'll go out now the war is won
With the whole world to explore,
We'll go out now the work is done
And you'll go back no more;
And I shall put my hand to the plough
As the independent do,
But I'm not so independent now —
But I don't mind, since it's you.

When you come home with the Battery
Come home from the Great War

When you come home with the Battery
All on the English shore;
At the time when the roses are pink and
red,
In the early days of June,
I might, perhaps, do what you said
And have a honeymoon.

May wrote:

And I can still feel the wind that blew up
from the Harbour, and smell the salt tangy
smell and hear the gulls crying as we came
to the house at Fowey, and he said,
'Darling we have come home'. He had
always loved home. We helped a little in the
orchard garden, rowing over in the old red
boat; and sailed out to sea in *True Tilda*
and met a small gale . . . We went to a party
where he was surrounded by people who
loved him and who welcomed me. We
dined in the Haven and there was silver
and wine in tall glasses and candle-light,
and across the table he smiled at me. And
then it was over . . . He had asked me to
stay on a little with his mother and sister;
his father was due back in Cambridge and
they were to travel to London together by
the night train, so I said goodbye to him
that winter evening at the door of The

Haven and went back to the quiet drawing room and lamplight and the sound of the sea washing the rocks below the garden wall.

To commemorate her two weeks with Bevil, May wrote the following poem.

English Leave

Kneel then in the warm lamplight, O my Love,
Your dear dark head against my quiet breast,
And take me in your arms again and so
Hush my tired heart to rest;
And say that of all glories you have won
My love's most dear and best.

Only tonight I want you all my own,
(Tomorrow I will laugh and bid you go,)
That if these fourteen days of heaven on earth
Are all the love-time we shall ever know
I may remember I am yours: My Dear,
Hold me still closer, still . . . and tell me so.

After his leave, Bevil travelled back to Germany to join his Battery. It was very cold and he wrote:

(30th January) The train rolled into Düren at 7am this morning . . . so I caught the train out there to Langerwehe . . . It has been pretty hard weather here all the time and people are skating and the ground is all white with snow and it is snowing now . . . I must go out and see Peggy and Funny Face and all the other horses.

(31st January) Peggy and Funny Face send their love and are very annoyed because the ground remains so hard they can only go for walking exercise . . . I have arranged for Peggy to be sent to England to be sold. I did this so that I could then follow up the history of her wanderings and know her new home while if she is left on the continent it is a toss up.

(2nd February) I have visions of being with you about the 25th of this month. I am writing to try and book my old rooms at Cambridge Terrace from 3rd March . . . I had a long letter from Fergus. He expects to be demobilised very shortly and I shall try and get him to live with me until 3rd

June [the day May and Bevil had fixed for their wedding]. I am writing this in bed as I am very lazy, having caught a small chill. I have stayed in bed for breakfast; when one lived in holes in the ground I never caught chills which seems rather silly. It must have been the sudden change. It has been freezing here without a break for 14 days and the ice on the ponds is very, very thick.

This was Bevil's last letter.

On 5th February 1919 the War Office informed Q and May that Bevil was dangerously ill with pneumonia following flu but permission to visit was not granted.

Sister R Dalzell sent word to Q on 5th February:

I am sorry to tell you that your son is lying seriously ill in this hospital. He was admitted with flu and since then pneumonia has developed. He became rapidly worse during the day and tonight his condition gives us the gravest anxiety. He has a high fever and is very delirious. You may be perfectly certain that everything possible is being done for him and that he will have every possible care and attention

. . . I am very sorry to be the bearer of such bad news but hope tomorrow to be able to send you a better report, though I am afraid I dare not give you too much hope as he really is very seriously ill tonight.

The Sister wrote again on the following day:

Long before you receive this letter you will have had the news of your son's death. He died with us this morning at 7am and he was very ill and delirious all night and became rapidly worse. It is so awfully sad to think that a big strong cheery man, as he seems to be, should go so quickly, especially as he had gone through the War so successfully, as he told us, with only slight wounds. His death has cast a gloom in the officers' ward, some of the other patients knew him personally and this has been a great shock to them . . . He was awfully pleased with a bit of white heather which he had received from Cornwall yesterday morning. He was wearing it in the buttonhole of his pyjamas jacket.

May wrote:

On the night of the 7th we were sitting by the fire before dinner. My Father, I remember, had just said, 'No news is good news,' hoping to hearten me, when the maid came in with a telegram on the silver salver from the hall. I got up. She tried to pass me to hand it to my Father, but I knew, and with blazing certainty, that I must open it myself, that this last was between, and only between, him and me. A voice I didn't know said, 'I think that is for me,' and I took it from the silver disc as she turned and ran. The War Office regretted that Major B B Quiller-Couch had died of pneumonia in the early hours of the morning of 6th February. Actually I had known it for some time, but I had still hoped. Now there was no hope. It was the end of the world.

Death

Lord, since you let him die and did not save
My own dear Love for me,
And since my heart has gone to him
Over in Germany,
I only have one prayer to make
To you for him and me.

That you will give him in your Heaven
(Dear Lord, I know him well),
Neither the harps nor floors of gold
Of which I have heard tell,
Nor jasper nor onyx palaces,
Nor fields of asphodel.

Give him some windy seaport town
With cliffs and tumbled shores,
And a swift boat with big brown sails;
And a great pair of oars;
And a wind sweet-scented from the
land,
And the sun bright on grey tors.

Give him a horse to ride, bare fields,
And the dear friends he knew,
And in the springtime flowers to find
And distant hills, all blue;
And violets for the memory
Of things we used to do.

Give me June roses when I go
To meet him, for the rest,
That he, young, splendid, strong, may
crush
Red roses to my breast,
And kiss my lips again, and so
Find love in Heaven best.

The Battery telegraphed to say that they were waiting for Q and May to say when they could arrive for the funeral. But when Q and May arrived at the War Office in London they were refused permission to go. And May wrote:

So they buried him over in Germany on 11th February and 400 men from his Battery, and his friends from the Staffs and the other formations he had known followed him on that last journey; and his Captain, who loved him, and his Senior Subaltern who had been with him since 1916 and adored him, acted for us — we were not there — and how does one forgive?

We came home to Fowey in the early hours of the morning. (I had rung my father). There was a grey sky and a grey sea and the waves leapt and dragged at the rocks below the garden. What came into my head was, 'And many waters cannot quench love'; and on that I went in to find his mother.

I was there for some time. I think the whole town mourned for him. They had known him as a small boy in a red beret rowing his dinghy about the harbour, going fishing with Groze the boatman, sailing with his sister and his Oxford friends. He had a smile, they said, and a greeting for everyone, and in the war when he came on leave, a man grown and with responsibilities heavy upon him and the knowledge of war, there was still the same smile and the same kindly question of how things were with them; the same invincible cheerfulness. The wind blew in salt from the sea, and at night, looking from my window, I could see the riding-lights of the ships in the harbour, and the lights in the windows of Polruan across the water. The stars came out and hung above the hill, and dawn came and the ships put out their riding-lights, and the windows went blank and the stars faded — and he would never come home any more.

After

Dear, since it was for England that you died
Who so adored her, I will love her still;
But when all's hushed save lapping of the tide
And lights are yellow on Polruan hill,
You'll understand

That since I cannot reach to you my
hand
And say 'how beautiful', and after say,
'We have been very happy all today',
My love for her has grown a little sad:
And though, remembering, I will be glad
When all the ships hang out their
riding-lights,
I shall not count them now that you are
dead,
But wonder what you do in Heaven o'
nights
And lift my eyes beyond the hill instead,
And wonder which of all the stars I see
Is the new star you have hung out for
me.

Captain T Marshall wrote to Q after the
funeral:

We were all very sorry indeed you were
unable to get out for the funeral. We buried
the Major with full military honours, one of
my own black teams from my section
pulling the gun-carriage. There were a large
number of wreaths, the Battery giving the
largest for it had to be carried by two men.
Peggy, his mare, was led behind by his
groom with the boots reversed in the
stirrups, while his belt and cap were fixed

Bevil's grave as it was when he was buried
in Duren Military Cemetery
(by courtesy of Trinity College, Oxford)

to the top of the coffin. Marshall and I were the chief mourners, and there were nearly 400 officers and men besides who came to see our Major laid to rest. As I suppose you know the Major and I were practically contemporaries in the Battery. In all I served under him for over two years, and I can never hope to serve under a better Battery Commander in action. He and I remained with the Battery through every battle since September 1916 and now only I am left. He was much more to me than my Battery Commander, and the Battery will never be quite the same now he has gone.

OBITUARY — *THE TIMES* — 11th February 1919

QUILLER-COUCH. On the 6th Feb, at Düren (Army of Occupation), of pneumonia, MAJOR BEVIL BRIAN QUILLER-COUCH MC, RFA, aged 28.

MAJOR BEVIL B QUILLER-COUCH, MC, RFA whose death was announced in *The Times* yesterday, died at Düren on February 6, of pneumonia, aged 28. The only son of Sir Arthur and Lady Quiller-Couch, of The Haven, Fowey, Cornwall and of Cambridge, he was educated at Winchester and at Trinity College, Oxford where he was captain of the Boat Club and a notable oar. He stroked in the OUBC Trial Eights in 1911 (losing) and 1912 (winning). His opponent stroke in both races was his friend Reggie Fletcher, who fell early in the war. Quiller-Couch also won the University Pairs in 1912 (with H R Munday) and 1913 (with C E Tinne) and in the latter year rowed with Tinne, in the final for the Goblets at Henley. At Oxford he joined the OTC (Artillery) and passed into the Special Reserve. He went to France in August 1914, as a second lieutenant in the 2nd Division and continued in active service with that Division throughout the war, gaining the MC and two mentions in dispatches with a temporary majority. He had commanded the 9th Battery, 41st Brigade, RFA for two and a half years, and finally led it with the Army of Occupation to Langerwehe, near Düren where he died. His engagement to May Wedderburn, daughter of Mr and Mrs C Cannan, of Magdalen Gate House, Oxford was recently announced in *The Times*.

Many of Bevil's fellow officers were deeply affected by his death as is apparent from the following extracts taken from letters written to Sir Arthur and Lady Quiller-Couch.

From Brigadier General Sanders, RA:

> He was quite one of the best officers in the Division. Very gallant, always cheery and full of energy, he was most popular with everyone with whom he had dealings. He had also quite exceptional abilities which would have carried him far in the Army and I expect in any other profession. He was a really good all round soldier and man and his death is a very bitter grief and loss to every one of us. You will be glad to know that it was a great joy to him to hear that his name had gone in for a very well earned DSO.

And from Captain T Marshall:

> I can assure you it is the hardest blow that has been struck against this Battery during the whole War, particularly coming as it did after the fighting had ceased and one thought all danger passed. It was all so sudden that it is still hard to believe that we shall not again have our beloved Major at the head of the Battery . . . When I received the news that he had passed away it was the

greatest shock of my life to think that one so full of energy who had lived through more than four years of a life when from day to day one thanked God to be alive, to see the dawning of the day, had been suddenly taken from our midst.

Fulfilment

Dear, since you've gone across the other side
(Beyond the stars, men say), you'll wait for me
Who only wish I also could have died,
And ask of God that he
For love will make the waiting not too long:
And if I'm old
And you still young and strong,
And all the laughter has gone from my eyes
And from my hair the gold;
You will devise
Quickly some way to come to me, and fold
Me in your arms again, and kiss away
The loneliness that breaks my heart today.

And afterwards, since God is very kind
And we have only had our twenty days,
Perhaps together he will let us find
Down the blue waterways
The wedded love we had no time to
know:
And if I'm sad
(And you loved laughter so),
You'll kiss my lips to laughter back again,
My eyes to make them glad;
Until the pain
That is a sword across the joy we had
Is but a flame of glory in our bliss,
The dear true passion of our lovers' kiss.

Young Adventure

I know why I've grown old: it is because
you died
Splendidly young: and when you went
away
My youth went with you, lest you should
ride one day
On some new high adventure, and
beyond any friend
Your heart call mine (because the way
was long,
Because the way was hard), who

dreamed me strong
To kiss goodbye and bless the journey's
end.
And if my youth had stayed on earth
with me,
With me who am so very tired and sad
(So tired that April cannot make me
glad,
That bugles in the morning break my
heart),
I might (though I would also play my
part
Bravely, since you once called me very
brave)
Kiss with less courage than I used to do.
My heart you had, my life, and when you
died
I became old: I sent my youth with you.

Lionel Buxton, who had commanded the 36th
Brigade, Ammunition Column, described
Bevil thus:

Quiller was the first man to teach me that
cheeriness, wit and humour went hand in
hand with all the miseries of war, and
though we had hard times together the fact
of being with Quiller made the hardest
times into happy ones. I cannot say how
distressed I am at losing such a dear friend,

and it is indeed hard that Quiller whom I believe had the finest regimental record of any gunner in the BEF should go out after all was over and just when a happy home life was opening before him.

THE OXFORD MAGAZINE
— 14th FEBRUARY 1919

The death of Major Bevil Quiller-Couch, who died in Germany last week after a few days' illness, saddens two Universities, and falls with terrible weight on some of our very oldest and best friends. Among the foremost in the War, as he had been here, in promise and prowess, Major Quiller-Couch had come through all its years with single and increasing distinction, and was looking forward to returning shortly to civil life, in which he had every prospect of happiness and success, when he was cut off by that fatal scourge, pneumonia. No words can express the tragedy of such an ending. We hardly like to attempt any, yet we could not leave our sympathy and condolence quite unsaid.

It is indeed so tragic, so ironic, so appallingly sad that Bevil could survive fighting continuously for over four years during the war only to end up dying, in Germany, on foreign land far from his loved ones, and when he had less than two weeks to go before demobilisation. It is also ironic that he had waited until the end of the war before asking May to marry him because he didn't want her to worry about him during the war (perhaps he didn't think he would survive the war?). This meant that in the end they had very little time together.

A Letter

Summer in England! O My Dear,
I only wish that you were here:
The sky is very blue,
And there's the river blue and green
With amber-coloured lights between
To float a small canoe:
And there's a willow-tree for shade,
And tea and bread and marmalade,
Pale orange, for us two.

Do you know how the river runs
Far, very far, from Flanders' guns
Between the fields of hay?
Right up above the Grey Stone Pool
Where the swift water tumbles cool

We might have gone today:
Gone past the weir above the Bridge,
And seen the sun on Hinksey ridge,
And water-rats at play;

For once forgot the tides that break
Against our hearts, forgot to shake
The world, forgot to dream:
And seen the river running by
The hills, mist-muffled, next the sky
That all untrodden seem:
And when the shadowed evening came
With dripping paddles sun-aflame
Dropped homewards with the stream.

Last night behind the apple-tree
There was a baby moon to see,
Silver and very far:
And there were wallflowers drooping
down
To sleep, gay wallflowers gold and
brown,
And the dark deodar:
The lilac, pale — you know the way
Of a hot English night in May.
There came one little star . . .

AFTER THE WAR

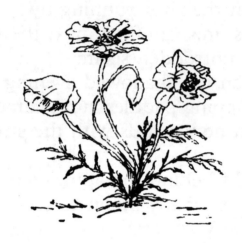

May wrote:

When I got home there was a question mark against the future. Watching the lights over Polruan I had told myself that there was France left; France where we had been happy; France of whose history we had been for a small time a part; I thought of the refugees about whom Bevil had written, making their way across the Somme Battlefields, and I thought that if I could help to repair that desolation, that would be something; but coming home on a cold March evening to a house that had suddenly grown old and sorrowful and tired, I knew that here in England were also two houses made desolate and that France could not be.

May had her whole life stretching before her but she had lost her man and the desolation must have been immense. She wrote the following poems pouring out her grief. Writing such verse must have helped her to come to terms with her loss.

At Dawn

All night I tossed, troubling my heart
What next with life to do:

161

Wond'ring what you would wish, and
could not sleep
The long dark through:
But when the dawn came very still and
cold,
Painting the window blue,
And the new hope went out to meet the
old,
My heart was hushed and knew
(Though you are dead and all our love is
vain
Heart of my Heart, to bring you back
again)
That first of all things left for me to do,
Though you are dead, is simply to love
you.

Stars

We looked at Orion one cold night —
Very still in the blue
Were the stars that are his Belt and
Sword,
The only stars I knew —
The stars that God set in His sky
Ages ago for you,
Since you were a soldier lover, and died,
And a girl gave her heart to you.

A New Song

It's very far from Waterloo
To Rouen in the rain,
Southampton over to Le Havre
Where the Drafts entrain:
It's not so far for loving hearts
To fields of Picardy,-
I took some roses to a man
That his girl gave to me.
    Pull out, pull out from Waterloo,
    Our hearts have gone before,
    We'll thank the little gods who send
    Us nearer to our War:
    It's not so far from Rouen town
    To fields of Picardy —
    I've seen the wounded men come down
    To sleep in Normandy.

It's very far from Waterloo
Out to the cruel Rhine,
It's farther still to Heaven's Gate
For sad hearts like mine:
Victoria, Folkestone and Boulogne,
The way all lovers know —
We used to see our men go out,
But they'll not let us go.
    Pull out, pull out from Waterloo,

Our hearts have gone before,
We'll thank the gods that give us
jobs
To tidy up the War:
And English loves sleep soft and
sound
In kindly Picardy —
But my Love lies in lonelier ground
Over in Germany.

It's very far from Waterloo
To London where they dance,
It's not so far from Heaven's Gate
Across in broken France:
Southampton over to Le Havre,
We used to know the way —
We used to see the Drafts go up
Where we'll go up today.
    Pull out, pull out from Waterloo,
    We'll get back to our war,
    Our hearts are over with our men
    Who will come back no more:
    And English loves sleep soft and
    sound
    In kindly Picardy —
    But my Love lies in lonelier ground
    Over in Germany.

164

Soldier-Love

Time will fold all our darling love away,
The beauty and the splendour that was
ours
Will later lovers take to light their day,
And wear for one another our own
flowers.

But far beyond the passion Paris knew
Hot-footed on the journey to blown Troy,
They'll hold the love of soldiers such as
you
Who gave the Generations back to joy.

May wrote:

I was fortunate because though I had lost
everything I kept so much. I did not believe
that the Dead had died for nothing, nor
that we should have 'kept out of the War'
— The Dead had kept faith, and so, if we
did not grudge it, had we. They had gone
to War because of a 'Scrap of Paper' and
because of England, and they had saved the
'Scrap of Paper' and they had saved
England, and if we were wise enough, the
world.

When I Shall Come

When I shall come through all the world
at last
Upon some evening late,
And Peter ask me what I did on earth
That he should open for me Heaven's
gate,

I shall not try to think of all the things
I did, and failed to do,
But put my hands against my heart that
is
A brown bird singing at the thought of
you,

And say I was a woman, and I gave
One man all love I had,
And he went out to the Great War and
died,
But since I loved him was made very
glad.

And Michael, who is leader in God's wars,
Will take the golden key
And say, 'I know her Soldier, let her in',
And turn the lock, and swing the door
for me.

And the great angels will lift up their swords
For me as I go through,
And turn back to their watch again, and I
Shall hold your hands and be again with you.

If I Had Died

If I had died instead of you
For whom are all my tears
You who loved very greatly would have made
A glory of your years
And when we two met in the Afterwards,
As surely we shall meet,
Have brought them with the love you held
And put them at my feet.

Bevil received the DSO posthumously and it was gazetted on the 3rd June 1919, the day he was to have married May:

Captain (A/Major) Bevil Brian Quiller-Couch MC. RFA, SR has invariably shown marked initiative, energy and resource;

untiring and cool, never sparing himself. Can always be relied on to 'get things done' under adverse conditions. Served at the front continuously since 1914.

At Q's house silence descended upon the devastated household and Q took a house on Dartmoor to be away for a while. He wrote to his sister Lilian:

3rd June was to have been dear Boy's wedding day and we always celebrated 'days' in the old time. (If a man thought himself important enough to be the sport of the Gods, I might have felt worse than I did — and it was bad enough — to pick up the paper yesterday morning of all days and read Boy's DSO in the Birthday List). For me, I have a wild desire to get home and plunge into writing a book. Up here I just work all the time and go to bed dog-tired. I find I have it all my own way here — now that I don't care. The new Tripos is an established success. It will double its number in 1920 and should double again in 1921.

After Bevil's death, it was arranged that Peggy, his field charger, would be bought by the Quiller-Couch family so that she could live the rest of her life at Fowey. Captain T Marshall arranged for Peggy to be transported to England and wrote to Q:

> Now about Peggy, I have taken her under my care for the time being as I expected you would want her. Unfortunately the blow [Bevil's death] fell before all the necessary documents were completed in the case, but all we want is for you to send the name of someone who will attend the public auction in England. Then we can arrange to have the mare sent home in due course. The person nominated to buy the mare will then be informed and bid for her in the auction ring. Your name will be scissor-clipped on her on the near side under the saddle. I am pleased to think that she is going to be well cared for as she is a beautiful mare in spite of her four and a half years active service.

Thus Peggy was acquired and was eventually brought down to Fowey and looked after by Foy. Q, having seen Peggy in London, wrote to Lilian, his sister:

> Peggy is at present at livery opposite Marble Arch. Whether or not she detected something familiar in my footstep when I

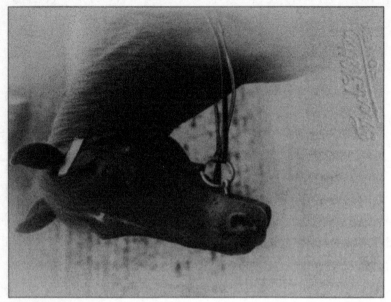

Peggy, Bevil's charger
(by courtesy of Jim Slater)

Bevil Quiller-Couch

went into the loose box, she was waiting for me. Took no notice of the stableman, but came straight to me, snuffled me all over the chest and then bent down her neck like 'Royal Egypt'. While I stroked her, she nuzzled my wrist and back of my other hand, as if kissing it over and over: and when I turned about to speak to the Manager, her nose came pushing through between my arm and body, kind of insisting that I hadn't made enough love to her. It sounds silly, but it seemed as if the creature really did know something and was trying to say it.

Peggy lived out the rest of her life at Fowey. When she died Q had her photograph hung just below one of Bevil in uniform, in his sitting room at Jesus College. And if a visitor were to ask a question about the two photographs, Q would answer very quietly or be so overcome with emotion he would have to leave the room. Q also had one of Peggy's hoofs made into an inkwell.

Meanwhile May continued to write and to grieve.

Possession

They tell me I possess my heart
Most marvellous quietly; that's not true,
Because I gave my heart away,
My Very Dear, to you:
And being so possessed I know
The strength your brave heart knew.

Courage

When Hope was fled,
Then Courage came, and said,
'I will lift up your head,
Who with Love watched the bed
Of your dear Dead,
And he go comforted.'

An Old Song

There are so many of us now,
I and you and you —
Who need's must set our teeth and face

Whatever life may do, may do,
Whatever life may do.

They think us hard because we laugh,
I and you and you —
Our men went laughing out to die
So how else should we do, we do,
So how else should we do?
But when these Happy are not near
Then I and you and you —
May break our hearts and weep our loves
As any girl must do, must do,
As any girl must do.

(Q wrote, 'I love *An Old Song* by the way, and can't tell you why; which is the best of all reasons'.) In the months after Bevil's death Q was also finding life difficult. He wrote to a friend:

I have been rather heavily overworking at Cambridge and later at Oxford on examination work. It deadens pain. But I begin to see that it were better — and braver — to face the pain and 'have it out'. For by shirking it, one's whole mind gets deadened. Really I don't care, half my time, what happens in a world that has killed my dearest and most natural hope.

Bevil's death had affected Q so badly that he couldn't trust himself to write about it (or indeed talk about it). The wound that it had inflicted on his heart never healed completely. As he encouraged May to write verse, he confessed that poetry had given up on him. 'For years I've started a poem called Paradise':

In Paradise there is a lake,
Hart and roe with gentle eyes
Haunt to it at eve to slake
Their thirst, in Paradise.

But he could never write more than this one verse. Paradise was no more for him.

To Certain Men

*Who were old in a time of War and
held belief in Young Love*

You had met Life and Death before
We reached our proven days,
You said the things that kept our hearts
Unhurt in Beauty's ways.

You did not lift your hands and cry
Shame on our young estate,

Nor hold we were, as many held,
Weak, vain, degenerate.

You saw the world your manhood made
Go crashing down to dust,
And give us for our steadying
Ungrudgingly your trust.

You who will never see your sons'
Sons take their heritage,
Give us your grief to go with us
In the long wars we wage.

You know the Dream to which we hold
In our most lonely state,
And from your sorrow turn to us
Whose hearts are desolate,

And tell us that there is no life
For memory too long,
That Love is always with the Loved,
The Battle to the Strong,

And keep belief in our young love,
Whereby, made doubly sure,
We hold the pledge our Lovers gave
Through which we go secure.

May must have written this poem with Q very
much in mind.

Sir Arthur Quiller-Couch
(by courtesy of Guy Symondson)

Women Demobilized

July 1919

Now must we go again back to the world
Full of grey ghosts and voices of men
dying,
And in the rain the sounding of Last
Posts
And Lovers' crying —
Back to the old, back to the empty world.

Now are put by the bugles and the
drums,
And the worn spurs, and the great
swords they carried,
Now are we made most lonely, proudly,
theirs,
The men we married:
Under the dome the long roll of the
drums.

Now are the Fallen happy and sleep
sound,
Now in the end, to us is come the
paying,
These who return will find the love they
spend,

But we are praying
Love of our Lovers fallen who sleep
sound.

Now in our hearts abides always our war,
Time brings, to us, no day for our
forgetting,
Never for us is folded War away,
Dawn or sun setting,
Now in our hearts abides always our war.

May wrote:

What one needs most in shock and grief is
time. Losing one's world, one still wanders
in it, a ghost. It is for long, more real than
the new world into which one knows (but
does not want to know) one must presently
move and live.

The Song Royal

All beauty and all glory I have known:
The steadfastness of stars: and gentleness:
The young clean courage of the hill-born
streams:
The tenderness of twilight: daffodils:
The joy of apple orchards: the sea winds

Strong in the sails of ships: June's happiness,
June shyly proud fulfilling Winter's dreams.
Dawn on the downs: the sure strength of the hills:
The everlasting comfort of the sea:
All these are mine because you have loved me:
All these you loved, and dying, gave to me.

All beauty and all glory I have known:
True love: which is unshaken happiness:
And courage: in the splendour of our days:
And tenderness: in the dear things we said:
And truth: in your true kisses on my lips:
And safety: in your heart's strong gentleness:
And faith: in the sure faith of our love's ways:
And hope: in our new hope that was the old:
And joy: in our love's utter certainty:
All these are mine because you still love me:
All these, though you are dead, you give to me.

In the late summer of 1919 May went back to work at the Oxford University Press, helping to edit the *Oxford Magazine* which came out weekly.

She recorded:

> In my morning's post came a letter, an official letter from R W Chapman. The Press, the Delegates, he wrote, hoped that I would come back to work for them. My old desk waited for me and they would all be more than glad to have me again . . . I needed a job. I knew well enough that the only antidote to pain is work and I loved the Press . . . I knew the *Oxford Magazine*. It had always appeared weekly in our house. Father had been one of its early Editors and Q had been his right hand man . . . I accepted with grateful thanks and went back almost at once.

A Dream House

I will build me a house some day,
In the days when I am old,
And I will have warm-hearted fires
To keep me from the cold;

And it shall be between the sea
And the lift of the English wold.

And I will have sun-dazzled lawns
With roses on each side,
And roses red and white to climb
My windows opened wide
That I may hear the seagulls call
And the lapping of the tide.

And there shall be quiet garden paths
And lilies at the gate,
And evening primroses to light
Lamps when the hour is late;
Lest in the dark they pass my doors
For whom I watch and wait.

And I will have sad marigolds
For the dear dreams that die,
And white-starred saxifrage to speak
Of hills and open sky,
And speedwell round my garden's edge
To greet the passer-by.

And I'll have heather for the loves
That linger north of Tweed,
And lavender and rosemary
For such as are in need;
And to crown all, upon the wall,
Garlands of Oxford Weed.

And to my house shall come the friends
I laughed with long ago,
And all who labour where the winds
That break men's high hopes blow;
And they shall rest and hardly hear
Rose petals dropping slow.

And the long splash of breaking waves
Shall hush them night and day,
Until the restless strength returns
To send them on their way,
And they shall call goodbye and go
As those whose hearts are gay.

The Golden Age

We were very young and in love with life
Five years ago;
Eighteen, nineteen, twenty, and twenty one
(And the years all go):
And love was ours and the world lay
under our hands,
And we laughed that it was so.

We were very young and in love with joy
Before the war;
Golden lovers we had, splendid and true
(They went to the War):

And love was ours and life lay under our hands,
And we kissed and asked no more.

We were very young, we were very wise,
For love is best;
Beauty and youth we lost, and then our loves
(For Death took the best):
And life is ours and all we ask is life's ending,
To find them and so have rest.

May mourned deeply for Bevil, despite the distractions of a job. She wrote:

It was lonely. It was lonely because I went to work and came home again alone; and to a house which dear as it was to me and God knew how dear, could never be the one to which he would come; never his and mine.

When The Vision Dies . . .

When the Vision dies in the dust of the market-place,
When the Light is dim,

When you lift up your eyes and cannot
behold his face,
When your heart is far from him,
Know this is your War; in this loneliest
hour you ride
Down the Roads he knew;
Though he comes no more at night he
will kneel at your side,
For comfort to dream with you.

Splendid Days

These were the Splendid Days,
And they are fled,
Now go we lonely ways,
Our Loves are dead:
Only the vision stays
And the word said.

Now never Splendid Days
The years will bring,
Now go we lonely ways
Remembering:
Still with the Lover stays
The given ring.

May had her second volume of poetry, *The
Splendid Days*, published in 1919 and it was

dedicated to Bevil. Many of her saddest poems were included in this volume, such as 'Death', 'Fulfilment', 'After', 'The Song Royal', 'At Dawn', and 'When the Vision Dies' and also some of her most joyous poems such as 'The Armistice', 'Paris November 1918', 'For a Girl', 'Paris Leave', 'Now I will Make New Happy Songs' and 'English Leave'.

Sir Walter Raleigh had written earlier to May about *The Splendid Days*: 'It is heart-breaking. Almost terribly naked — the record parts of it, I mean those poems about the news. I think you should publish it, if a book is published it's off your mind and can look after itself, whereas, if you keep it in a desk it's an anxiety.' And *The Splendid Days* was reviewed in the *Bookman*:

If you have read Miss Cannan's earlier book of verse, *In War Time*, you will know that she has imagination, a gift of clothing ordinary things with the magic of poetry, but none of her other songs are so poignant, so charged with feeling and emotion as are some in this new volume . . . The very poetry of sorrow is in these verses, but there is so much beauty of thought and feeling that they touch and uplift more than they sadden one.

185

The following poem is from a collection of unpublished verses by May Cannan.

To The Germans 1919

You boasted you had won until the last
Slow-dawned invincible November day;
You boasted that we never should forget
The Terror of your way:
You have no power on us for whom our
loves
Bought all Tomorrow with their Yester-
day.
You have no power on us, although you
took
Death and despair to minister your hate:
You cannot shake the peace wherein we
go
Always inviolate
The peace our lovers, dying, bought for
us,
That knows you not: it is beyond your
hate.

May's opinion of the Germans very much reflected the mood of the day which was very anti-German. Bevil's opinions on the Germans were expressed in some of his letters home. As a soldier, he had to believe in the stupidity and in the evil of the enemy although nowadays, obviously, these feelings would be seen as politically incorrect. Some short extracts from his letters follow:

(11/10/15)
I saw such a priceless Bosche I could have hit him with a stone and with my telescope he might have been in the next room. I could read the number on his cap quite plainly too. He was very ugly. We have been firing at a gap between the Cottages where they walk across the open; about 12.30pm yesterday we noticed one going across with something white under his arm. Today at almost the same time he appeared again but was a bit too slow so something white still lies on the ground between the Cottages and we think it was the Tablecloth for dinner being taken to the Officers' Dug Out.

(19/6/15)
I had a great shoot at a Church the other day . . . I had a dozen rounds at it and got six into the roof, two into the tower and one into the West end. The Bosche had been observing from it and he was well

gingered up in the brick dust, which was very satisfying.

(16/3/16)

We saw hundreds of Bosche with our telescope. Two days ago I went up a mountain before dawn and stayed there gazing until 12.30pm. I saw the Bosche Generals going for a canter to improve their livers and a girl leading a cow, women hanging out washing in the cottage gardens, trains puffing up and down. All this and many other interesting things in the distance. Nearer, there were Bosches cooking their breakfasts and the whole time seemed like an hour. The mountain too is very gruesome and I could have collected a sack full of any one particular bone.

(13/11/16)

We have been shooting hard ever since 5.45am and the battle has been raging in the densest of fogs . . . All round the Observation Post this morning were little groups of unattended Bosche walking aimlessly about in the fog and quite lost. When I pointed in the direction of the prisoners' collecting station they were much pleased and two or three said 'Thank you'. One thing about the fog, the Bosche hadn't the smallest idea what was happening and bombardments being so usual, I don't think even now he knows that he has been attacked say five miles east of the front line.

In October 1919 May was staying down in Fowey with the Quiller-Couches. May would ride Peggy while there. Foy rode Peggy's field companion, another charger ending her days at Fowey. May wrote:

I had written a poem called *Riding* and Q had wanted me to include it in *The Splendid Days* but I wouldn't, and now it is one that comes back often into my mind.

Riding

They brought the mare — I wondered if they heard
The beat of my heart, or saw the red blood stir,
Go from my face like a wave, or how my hands
Shook as I mounted her.

See, once he wrote, 'they are bringing the mare round now,'
And just sometimes I look for his letters still,
Forget he is dead: well, that's all life to me
Riding alone the hill.

The roads are narrow in Cornwall and set between
Stiff wind-cropped hedges that shelter as you ride;
They were sadder roads and bare that he knew in France
The poplars on each side . . .

He must have ridden her often, felt the lift
Of the sure swift strength moving between his knees,
And I came near him a second, riding so,
Dreams, but Love lives by these.

Dreaming I rode the hill and the wind came up
Salt and sharp, blowing the rain from the sea,
And I knew he had ridden thus the Menin Road,
Is that all lost to me?

Down I rode through the lanes where the arched trees meet
As swords of our wedding day above my head,
O lonely of heart, in the world our men are ours
So hold you comforted.

Out from the lanes to the sea, the sea that breaks
For a million years its heart on a lonely shore
Well that's the answer I think, and we who gave
To our Dead must give more.

Just for a moment the sea, then the road goes on
Over the ridge, O dreams are woken again,
But riding so in my heart I have ridden with him
The Menin Road in the rain.

October, Cornwall, 1919

Cropped stubble lies beneath the harvest moon
And glad the months' increase the country yields,

191

And the year turns quiet-hearted to her dreams,
And Autumn brings fulfilment to the fields.

Now through the woods go home the jingling teams,
Over the ford, blue water to their knees;
And heavy with their fruit, gold, red and brown,
In the hushed orchards stand the apple trees.

Now from the harbour in the frosty nights
Voices of sailor men drift lonelily;
Brave to the town-lights burns Orion's sword,
And kind the lights of fishing boats at sea.

Now are there left to us these lasting loves:
The tireless faith of the gold harvest days,
The labour of firm'd fruit, and sweet, hard wood,
The slow homecomings through October haze,

The friendly speech of yellow lamplight thrown
Out from the low, unblinded window pane,
The crackling of wood fires, the long hushed eves,
The nights that give us back our youth again.

That autumn of 1919 May's father became ill and suffered a stroke in November. Over-work, anxiety and the bitter blow of Bevil's death were too much for him and he died on the 15th December 1919.

Almost all the staff at the Press either attended his funeral or lined the streets between Magdalen Gate House and the Church of St Peter-in-the-East. As all the tributes show, Charles Cannan had inspired loyalty and affection in a large number of people. He was buried in Holywell. A year later, *The Times Literary Supplement*, reviewing the last edition of the Oxford University Roll of Service, said about the Press: 'Probably no European Press did more to propagate historical and ethical truth about the war. The death of its Secretary, Charles Cannan, has left an inconsolable regret among all those more fortunate Oxford men, old and young, who had the honour to be acquainted with one of the finest characters and most piercing intelligences of our time. He was a great man, and is alive today in the spirit of the institution which he enriched with his personality and his life.'

And Q, who also attended the funeral, had written to May:

Your last letter did its best to prepare us. But, oh my dear, if Bevil had lived! I never longed for him so much for you. He had strong arms.

And after the funeral Q wrote:

Many people sidled up and spoke to me. One said, 'You were a great friend, I know. I'll only say that, however sure of myself I could be in a quarrel, if it were given to Cannan to arbitrate and he decided against me, I should know that somehow I was in the wrong.' I reckon no man ought to ask for a finer thing than that to be said over him. But why could not these people have said it long ago and loudly? Another told me it was the greatest blow Oxford had suffered for years. Dear God, as if I wanted to learn that. And yet it was good to hear.

After her father's death, May's mother knew she had to give up the lease on Magdalen Gate House and much to May's regret they left Oxford in the early part of 1920.

May wrote:

> I was at Fowey for a time while Mother went to my sister. Q was very tired. He had been lecturing to enormous audiences at Cambridge, driving himself to give his brilliant best (and it 'killed thought a little' so he welcomed it) and in January had written to me, 'the supply of chairs gave out and some 50 young men and women seated themselves on the floor. It was a quaint sight and made me feel like some old boy of the middle ages with his disciples sitting at his feet.' In December he had given a public lecture in the Haymarket in London to 'an audience of 800, and another 250 turned away'. Now I found him with his *Art of Reading* in proof and beginning to work on the index. His eyes were troubling him so I took courage in both hands and took it away from him saying that I could do indexes; my Father had said so, and was grateful and proud that he let me. There was so little that one could do. We worked on the

'Farm' rowing across the harbour among the big ships in the red boat, and in the quiet chilly evenings sat over the fire with the logs crackling (and he came in one evening and said what fool has sawn all the logs for his study too long, and it had been me!) with the tall oil lamps lighting our books; and sometimes friends came in for bridge and he would welcome them, and then saying 'this is not a place for you, child,' carry me off to his small library at the end of the passage; candle-lit, eight in a row on the big table in the window where he worked — I would read or write, and presently he would get up and walk up and down the room talking about whatever he was working on, or sit a little with me by the fire. We had two griefs now to share.

A few weeks later May met her mother in Exeter. She was finding it difficult to settle after her husband's death and had thought of living there. In the event she decided it was too cold.

May wrote:

We went on to Penzance, and then, on an impulse to the Scillies. It was stormy weather and the little steamer that the islanders had bought when her mine-sweeping days were over rocked and bucketed for three hours while we sat on a plank balanced on two barrels; but in God's good time we came through those troubled waters and into the shelter of the little quay at St Mary's. We stayed for three weeks in a white washed cottage on the main street of St Hugh Town. Mother sketched and I lay on the warm turf under the whins and wrote poetry and sometimes, mercifully, slept.

May's grief remained inconsolable and this is reflected in her poetry, which she was writing a year after Bevil's death.

Love in the Hills

I had lost you in the valleys where they lean
Cheek to cheek, these happy lovers, in between
The oak leaves, with the foxgloves for a screen.

On the downs before an April day broke
blue
Found I once your footsteps darkling in
the dew
Then the sun burned, and his day took
me from you.

But at night among the great hills in the
rain,
With the mist a curtain pulled across the
plain,
In the darkness you were at my side
again,
Hand in hand among the great hills in
the rain.

A Long Time After

About the roadways of my heart
My friends shall come and go
There shall be tears and laughter
For them as they shall know,
And dreams with high adventure
set
So gallant and gay
And I will wear a sword again
And ride with them the way.

Within the gardens of my heart
Beside the happy streams
My friends shall wander and forget
The breaking of their dreams
And find the old songs that we made
Before the wonder died,
And Rosemary and traveller's joy
For token when they ride.

Within the chambers of my heart
My oldest friends and true
The men who made my earth for me
And set my hands thereto,
The women who kept watch with me
When dawn was very far
The friends who stormed the world with
me
To find a hidden star,

Shall lie them down before my fire
And hush them very still
And whisper that they saw a star
Climb high above the hill
And find a little comforting
Before they go their ways
And touch of hands for memory
That knew the splendid days.

Q wrote to May on the anniversary of Bevil's
death, 6th February 1920:

I can look back calmly at times and then I always see it as a very lovely life: quite clear and clean with no hazy sentiment around it: packed with love for a special few and with such a love for home that he would never rest until he had brought home any chosen one from his Wykehamist friends to you, last and best. And I really don't think a braver heart ever beat. You have read what his fellow officers say . . . For it wasn't as if he was insensitive to danger. I came through an abominable gale with him once, when he was five or six years old: and when we were safe at anchor and I took him down to the cabin and cut him some food — the water, even down there, washing about our ankles, he looked up (with his mouth full of sandwich) and said 'That was pretty bad, wasn't it? I thought it was very bad. I had about enough of it, at one time.' He had on that little oily coat and sou'wester . . . Well, we must be brave too, though it will take longer for some of us. My dear, you came into it all and made it far more beautiful. When I hold your dear hand I know how beautiful.

20 FEBRUARY 1920

Sir Arthur Quiller-Couch
The Haven
Fowey
Cornwall

Sir,

I have it in command from His Majesty the King to inform you, as next of kin of the late Captain acting Major Bevil Brian Quiller-Couch DSO, MC of the Royal Field Artillery (SR) that this Officer was mentioned in the following Despatches for gallant and distinguished service in the field.

From Field Marshal Sir John French dated 30th November 1915 and published in the supplement of the *London Gazette* of 31st December 1915 dated 1st January 1916.

From Field Marshal Sir Douglas Haig dated 8th November 1918 and published in the second supplement of the *London Gazette* of 4th dated 7th July 1919.

I am to express to you the King's high appreciation of these services and to add that His Majesty trusts that their public acknowledgement may be of some consolation in your bereavement.

I have the honour to be, Sir,

Your obedient Servant,
M O Graham, Colonel
Deputy Military Secretary

In 1920 May and her mother took lodgings in London for a time. May got permission, at the office where the official history of the war was being written, to type up the diaries of the formations with which Bevil had served. In due course she also typed up all the letters Bevil had written from the front to his parents.

Paris, 1921

They would take from me my Dreams
But them I hid away
To go with me to Paris Town
Upon an April day;
And I will keep them in my heart
Whatever they shall say.

They would take from me my Love,
But he will come with me
To walk again in Paris Town
Where once we used to be;
And he will walk there at my side,
And they will never see.

They would take from me my Pain,
But Pain is strong and old,
He followed me to Paris Town
When all the trees were gold;
And now he laughs between green
leaves,
Seeing that I grow old.

They would take from me my Joy,
That is a wounded thing
Comes limping home into my heart
For warmth and comforting;
But I will take all Paris Town
For his safe-harbouring.

I will go with these my Dreams,
My wounded Joy and Pain,
Along the laughing boulevard
Where bridges cross the Seine,
And meet my Love in Paris Town
And walk with him again.

For Some

In Flanders fields
The poppies blow
Blow white and red
It is so long, so long ago
We left our Dead
And other lovers now we know —
We have new lovers instead.

In Flanders fields the poppies blow
Blow red and white:
It is so long, so long ago
We kissed good night:
And other kisses now we know —
And it is our right.

In Flanders fields the poppies blow
Both white and red:
The crosses stand a-row a-row
Above our dead:
What matter where our feet may go
When all is said?

In early 1921 May and her mother went to
Italy and spent several months touring and
sightseeing.

Bevil's grave as it is today. Some time after the war his remains were moved to the South Cologne War Cemetery.

In Rome

One said
Why walk you day long with the Dead?
The Dead, they died:
Behold they at your side
Live, and have need of you.

O heart, 'tis true:
And yet, he did not know . . .
It was all very long ago.

May wrote:

We were staying in the Ludovisi Quarter
and I went, my first morning in Rome, past
the fountain playing in the Piazza del
Terme and found the Via Cavour and went
down it to look for the Forum. Everyone
has his own Forum, but I loved best that
which is left of Ceasar's temple and the
Waters of the Vestal Virgins. Rome wasn't
crowded then, and sometimes I went there
and sat on the stone lip of the cool green
water and was quite alone. I went to the
Colosseum and was devastated by the hate
and the horror that still lived in it. It cried
aloud that it had belonged to the Emperors

and that it still belonged to them, and that they were dead. I went to the Palatine and met a Swede who said anyone could guess Rome but no one could know her and everything went down with time, and that 2000 years on we should be guesswork too; and then I found the Appian Way. Until all England went up through the Menin Gate I suppose there was no road like it. Soldiers built the Appian Way and the Legions marched along it and it led out of Rome to Brindisi. I went to the Porta St Sebastian and when I got to the path that leads to the catacombs I looked back and the Forum was hidden and it was St Peter's that I saw crowning Rome. I rang the bell at the great door of the Villa Priorate di Malta and walked in the garden between the cypresses, and when I left I knew how Adam went out from Eden with Eve.

Now the Dawn Breaks

O heart all is not over, now the dawn
Breaks in the rain-washed roofs and it is day,
Two thousand years go down to quietness,

The young years wake and crowd the great highway.

O Heart all is not ended, in the dawn
The trumpets blow the banners are unfurled,
All that thou hast, ride out again,
And find the old brave beauty of the world.

In the Train

All the way through the night I heard them talking of Italy,
Beautiful names of Italy breaking the roar of the train,
I that have known the loves and the songs and the sorrows of Italy,
Wake my heart to a dearer Love finding my France again.
France, and the names that we knew, we and our lovers in Picardy,
Brave and beautiful names unlocking the doorways of pain,
I that have known the loves and the songs and the sorrows of Picardy,
Know the hands of my own true love finding my France again.

Italy helped May to come to terms with her loss and she realised there was a life ahead of her. There were two million surplus women now, so job prospects were not good but May was a determined and independent young woman. She wrote of her trip: 'It has been for me a pilgrimage; a joy and a sorrow.'

May's mother decided to settle in the South of France. May, on the other hand, had to find work and a home and moved to London. She worked for a while as a secretary at King's College, London, and later on was offered a job as Assistant Librarian at the Athenaeum, which she thoroughly enjoyed.

May wrote:

The Members were many and various. The Bishops, fewer than legend had led me to expect, only wanted theological works and, except that they became impatient when it took time to extract them from the shelves, gave me no trouble. The politicians came in at a quarter to four; before question time in the House. They wanted everything — information from Blue Books, passages from Hansard, odd bits of Colonial History; Mr Stanley Baldwin wanted, endlessly, histories of Worcestershire; and then came E V Lucas who was reported never to speak, escorted by Charles Graves [Robert Graves's father] who was on my Committee. On my knees at the end of the Library collecting books to take upstairs for cataloguing, I heard Richard (my boss) say 'If it is poetry my assistant will know' and, as I got to my feet, Mr Graves said, 'Mr Lucas wants to find a poem'. Trying to look intelligent, I asked what poem, but he did not know! He did not know its name, its author, its first line or its last line or *any* line. In despair, I asked, 'What is it about?' And Mr Lucas spoke: 'Immigrants', he said. Well, I was Scottish and it was one we had put into the *Tripled Crown* [an anthology of poems May and her sisters had collected and had published]. 'Is it,' I asked and the years rolled back — 'is it . . .

'From the lone shieling on the misty Island
Mountains divide us and a waste of seas,
Yet the blood is strong, and the heart is Highland,
And we in dreams behold the Hebrides.'

It was and my reputation was made. Mr Kipling came in. He was writing *The War History of the Irish Guards*, the regiment in which his boy had served, and he wanted several pieces of information which I found him. For some time he came in frequently, working very quickly, talking all the time, saying, 'That's wonderful, that's just what I wanted. Now can you find me this?' And always thanked me when we had done. I did not tell him how I had sorrowed at missing him when he came to stay with us and I had had to go back to school.

In December of 1922 I went down to Cambridge to see Q. It was cold, still weather; the cold of the East counties that eats into one's bones, but there was a moon and I do not remember feeling cold. He gave a dinner party for me that first night in his rooms in Jesus College, and I remember coming in through the College gateway from Jesus Lane into the first court and running up those seventeenth century stairs to the door that opened straight into his Keeping Room, and opening it onto a bright fire and books and flowers. We dined by candle-light. Next morning I was taken first to the kitchens to thank the chef for what had been a wonderful dinner, and then to see his Cambridge; the incredible beauty that is King's College Chapel, St John's Combination Room, the homely, friendly bustle of the Petty Cury Market which he said was like a scene in Verona; and then to sit quietly in his room. One of the three windows looked over the Court and to a small view of the Fellows' Garden where he had planted a rose — Réné André brought up from his beloved Cornwall. She had grown, he told me proudly years after, all over the wall and round the corners. And is still there — Q's rose. Dusk came gently to the windows as we talked and then there was a faint scuffling on the stairs. He moved uneasily, broke the thread of his talk and asked shyly (he was a very shy man) — 'Dear, do you think you could send them away?' I got up saying, 'Of course,' but not knowing who 'they' might be, or for what they might have come, or why they should go. With my back to the door which I had shut behind me I stood and looked down on a crowd of under-graduates sitting on the steps. They came, I knew, at all hours, bringing him their work, the things they had written, their troubles, and he kept for them an open door; but this evening was mine. I looked down on the upturned faces and said, 'He says to come back another time,' and there was a clatter as they got to their feet. I had known lost Edens myself! I said 'another time', and smiled at them. Then I said, 'You know, tonight it is my turn.'

We went later to a party at the Sorleys. Their son, Charles, the poet, had been killed at Hulluch in 1915 and Q had given me his book. I saw them in that Cambridge room through a blur because they looked at me so very kindly and Q's introduction had been simply, 'This is May'.

My sister, Joanna, who had meant to be a painter and of whom life made a writer, published that same December her first novel. It was the beginning of a long and distinguished career. Q wrote to me, 'I think *'Misty Valley'* a very fine performance.'

The Echo 1923

When we are dead and all the longing's over
We shall have rest from dreams of love of men;
We shall not know the bees are in the clover
Nor weep the Summers of our loving them.

When all our beauty's dropped to dust
and ashes
Our tears will be the crying of the wind
That shakes their windows in the
window-sashes;
They will not know the thoughts
whereby we sinned.

It will not matter then how red the roses
They strew upon the pathway of the
bride;
We shall not fear that look of ours
discloses
The cowardice of the smiles wherewith
we lied.

We shall have paid at last our debt to
Laughter,
It will not matter then if we are sad,
They will not know, a generation after,
We wept the children that we never had.

We shall go down, a legend of lost
sorrow,
We shall endure, a lilt of sunset songs;
The bitterness will all be dead tomorrow —
They will not know we knew we lived too
long.

The Memorial which stands outside the church in Fowey set up to commemorate the war-dead. It has upon it the names of 40 officers and men from the two world wars, all of whom made the supreme sacrifice.

For a Soldier

When you are dead it will not be the
birds
Will waken you:
Though Nightingale sings through
The dim beseeching blue
He will not trouble you.

You will not stir
Though pale above the fir
The young moon climb and spill
Through the faint daffodil
Of dusk her silver while the Thrushes
sing.
Oh not for wing
Of Lark that beateth upward to the blue,
Oh not for song
Of Thrush that singeth
In the lilac tree, nor wrong
That Curlew crieth from the hill
Will you reach to the blue,
Will you push Death from you.

You will sleep sound, so sound
In the deep secret ground,
That if I called I know you would not
come;

You would lie there quite dumb
In the dark empty earth, and never
move:
And if I called 'Love, love',
Only the wind would whisper in the tree,
You would not wake for me.

But this will tear your sleep
However deep:
Long after you are done
With Love, and Song, and Sun,
This, this, will reach you through the
heavy earth,
The sound of hooves on turf,
The rattle of the limbers. This will move
You at long last. O dearer than first love,
The sound . . . What sound? . . . What
sound? . . .
The Battery changing ground.

And when they're past, you'll sigh and
slide to sleep,
Deep . . . deep.
The Lark sings to High Heaven in the
blue:
It will not be the birds will waken you.

Q, who was rarely able to talk openly about
Bevil after his death, did speak on the fifth
anniversary of the Armistice:

217

There are few households in this land that this war has left without a domestic sorrow far more real, more natural, more abiding than any exultation over victory. All the old statues of victory have wings: but Grief has no wings. She is the unwelcome lodger that squats on the hearthstone between us and the fire and will not move or be dislodged.

In 1923 May's third volume of poetry, *The House of Hope*, dedicated to her father, was published and May wrote:

Surprisingly a large number of people wrote to me about it, among them a young man who signed himself PJS (Percival James Slater). He had written to me in 1922 about *The Splendid Days* from some obscure town called Walsall, but I remember it because he had been at Oxford and loved the river and had written, 'You might have been out there yourself with him, [Bevil] the way you have caught the old feeling of it all.' Now in 1924 he wrote to me again, 'I found your book at the Press Depot this morning and I want to meet you sometime, anywhere where a long walk can end with a proper tea. The book is sad. You still think that all the best of life was over five or six years ago. So do I, but I sometimes feel that it's not a philosophy that helps this twisted world of 1924.'

May agreed to meet PJ and wrote: 'After all, there are very few of us left. Let us be good to each other. Let's have a meeting.'

They met and May described PJ thus:

He was tall and had brown eyes. He wore loose brown tweeds and had a bull-nosed Morris two-seater and was nice to my dog. He had been in the OUOTC and in the TA before the War, and had fought in the War until he had been badly wounded and sent home. Eventually he had 'got back' by joining the RFC and serving in captive balloons. They had spotted for the guns and their balloons had been set on fire by enemy shelling which forced them to jump out of their flaming baskets in parachutes. I found out afterwards that, when he was with them, he had been given the DFC. He was now a solicitor.

May and Percival met just five times before he asked her to marry him. She was torn by doubt, agonising for an old love and an old loyalty. She was not in love with Percival but told herself that all love is good, that to give love, to assuage a sorrow to fill a need, could not be wrong, and she agreed to marry him.

May recorded:

I had of course written to Q and written with tears. He answered: 'Yes, my dear, I did want this, more than I ever let you know.' I think that without that blessing we might have lost each other but now I realised that great as was the strain on me, it was on him greater; he could not believe that this that had come to us might not also founder; that I might not change my mind.

There would in August be PJ's Territorial Camp. [He was serving in the Territorial Army, 6th Battalion, South Staffs]. 'Would you like us to be married before camp?' I asked. 'We could. You could get a special licence.'

He said, 'My dear,' and looking in his face I saw that I was right. I went up the next weekend to Walsall. He had a small, red brick, Victorian house on the edge of town . . . He took me to his Father's house where I was to stay. We were welcomed by my future step-mother-in-law and presently PJ's father came in. A tall, reserved man he looked unapproachable and withdrawn. A man of many affairs, he was head of the family firm of Solicitors and had been twice Mayor of the town in the difficult days of the war, represented the Midlands on the first Government Committee for Food Rationing, and had given invaluable help over settling strikes . . . And now we had to explain to him, and I knew it really fell on me, that we wished to be married in a fortnight. He knew nothing about me and PJ was the eldest and much loved son. It was easier than I expected. He had a small library and after dinner he took me there and I discovered that he loved books and that the romance of his life had been his years at Oxford. Sitting anxiously on the edge of an armchair, I told my story and learned that he too had known loss, for PJ's mother had been killed by a bomb during a Zeppelin raid on the town in 1916 as she went to discharge some duty as Mayoress, and he could understand and sympathise with our troubles. I was touched by his concern that this venture should be for my happiness too, and inexpressibly relieved to know that we should have his help and support.

And it so became, for we were married very quietly on 6th June 1924 (and it was the sixth time we had met) in the Church of St George on the top of Camden Hill

Percival James Slater
(by courtesy of Jim Slater)

under the shadow of Chesterton's Water Tower. And after the thunderstorm that broke over the city later, I gave my flowers to my sister, Dorothea, who had come up from Oxford to be with me. We drove through a rain-washed countryside and picnicked at the edge of a cornfield in the sun, happy to be at last quiet and together. It was dusk when we came to the small fishing pub where we were to stay for our five days before Camp. Waiting for a moment in the car while this strange man I had married came round to open the door for me, I was threatened by panic and then I remembered Q's benediction in the letter I had shown PJ (and he had said it must surely be the most beautiful letter in the world) and I got out of the car and smiled at him and put my hand into his . . .

Q had written his benediction in a letter to May:

You Gods, look down,
And from your sacred vials pour your graces
Upon my daughter's head . . .

The Lord can explain what the bond was between your father and me. For me there was nothing like it: and I used to think how sad it was that there must in the nature of things be an end. And then, an unheeding child, you came into the room at breakfast: and in that moment there was a new flower — a new miracle — beside the old one. I think I've tried to explain this before but I never can explain it or how much the dear desire means to me that you should be protected and happy for ever and ever. I think you must have read this craving often between the lines of my letters. Child and sweetheart, keep your noble soul able to love me always and may you walk in light to the end of your days.

Ever and ever
Father

Perfect Epilogue
Armistice Day 1933

It's when the leaves are fallen I think of you,
And the long boulevards where the ghosts walk now,

And Paris is dark again save for one great star
That's caught and held in the dark arms of a bough

And wonder, among them are two a girl and boy
Silent, because their love was greater than song,
Who whisper 'farewell' and whisper 'if it's for ever';
And did not know, poor ghosts, for ever could be so long.

It's when the leaves are fallen I think of you,
And if you're lonely too, who went with the great host;
And know that Time's no mender of hearts but only
Still the divider of Light and Darkness, Ghost.

May wrote:

It mattered to me of course what Q thought of my poems more than anyone except my father, but long years afterwards when we were all grown old Maurice Jacks (a dear friend) was to assure me that the best things I had written were in *The Splendid Days*; but that there must be added to them the *Perfect Epilogue* which had written itself suddenly in 1933 and which I sent to Q and he wrote and told me he had put it in his copy of *The Splendid Days*.

May and PJ lived happily married for over 40 years. They had one son, Jim. Sadly, May had three subsequent pregnancies but lost the baby each time. She continued to write poems, short stories and novels in the first ten years of her marriage. However only one novel, *The Lonely Generation*, was published by Hutchinson in 1934. It was semi-autobiographical, telling the story of Delphine and Bobbie, who died in action in 1915, shortly after asking Delphine to marry him.

And May wrote:

The stars sang for me; but it didn't last long. Perhaps it is true as Wilde wrote, that all men kill the thing they love. I had married a man who had sought and found me across time and space because he loved the things I wrote, but when my book was published I found he could not bear to look at it, far less to read it, and obviously hated to hear it mentioned. Long years after, he told me he was sorry he had had a 'thing about it' and about my writing — he could not tell why — and I said that it did not matter, which had become nearly true.

May gave up writing after *The Lonely Generation* and PJ's reaction. She wrote only a handful of verses which she tucked away at the back of a drawer.

PJ took command of his territorial Battalion from 1931 to 1935. By this time May and PJ had moved to a farmhouse with land situated west of Wolverhampton, just over the border in Staffordshire. May had decided that, since she couldn't write, she would devote herself to the land and to her animals. She kept hens, ducks and sheep, a donkey and was devoted to her dogs. In 1938 PJ raised and commanded the 428/59 Search Light Battery, RA until 1940. He became a Brigadier in 1941 and commanded the 50th Anti Aircraft Brigade through to 1944 and then the 41st Anti Aircraft Brigade.

PJ became ADC to King George VI in 1945 and then to the Queen from 1953 to 1955. Their son, Jim, married Jenefer and they have one daughter, Clara. May and PJ retired to a house in Pangbourne, Berkshire where PJ died in 1967.

From One Generation to Another

Because we watched awhile the lamps
That burn before the shrine;
Because we led, a little while,
The changing vanguard line;
Because we toiled, and left our work
To make another's gain,
Because we sowed, and might not reap,
And dreamed we toiled in vain;
Because our names have lived awhile
For that which we have done;
Remember us when we have gone,
Whose race is past and run.

Because you too will come and go
And hold yourselves forgot,
Leave us to dream that there are none
Who are remembered not.

May wrote:

I suppose most of us have the desire to leave something behind us when we go into whatever there is (or is not) beyond the void. I don't think I ever treasured any extravagant hope of leaving anything that would be remembered, but as the years have gone by and times changed I have been glad to think that at least I wrote a salute to my generation.

May and Foy, Bevil's sister, remained dearest friends in later years. In 1969 May wrote to Foy:

It is over 50 years ago now my dear, but through all my life, and I am 75 now, I think I have 'walked in light' as he [Q] prayed I would because of the love and affection I found in France and The Haven — 'And lights are yellow on Polruan Hill'.

May died in her sleep at her home in Pangbourne at the age of 80 in 1973. This poem was written five days before her death.

The Long Road Home

Body said to Spirit
'Be still now, be still —
Blood and Bone and Nerve and Sinew

229

We have done your will
Four score year and more —
Be still now, be still.'

Spirit said to Body
'Be still now, be still —
Blood and Bone and Nerve and Sinew
You have done my will
Four score year and more —
But one thing still.

Brain and Memory and Mind
Would leave some Thing behind —
For a little, little, space
Hold Heart's dying race —
Then still, be still.

May's autobiography, *Grey Ghosts and Voices*, was published in 1976.

We do hope that you have enjoyed reading this large print book.

Did you know that all of our titles are available for purchase?

We publish a wide range of high quality large print books including:
Romances, Mysteries, Classics
General Fiction
Non Fiction and Westerns

Special interest titles available in large print are:
The Little Oxford Dictionary
Music Book
Song Book
Hymn Book
Service Book

Also available from us courtesy of Oxford University Press:
Young Readers' Dictionary
(large print edition)
Young Readers' Thesaurus
(large print edition)

For further information or a free brochure, please contact us at:
Ulverscroft Large Print Books Ltd.,
The Green, Bradgate Road, Anstey,
Leicester, LE7 7FU, England.
Tel: (00 44) 0116 236 4325
Fax: (00 44) 0116 234 0205

GHOSTMAN

Kenneth Royce

Jones boasted that he never forgot a face. When he was found dead outside the National Gallery it was assumed he had remembered one too many. The man he had claimed to have identified had been publicly executed in Moscow some years before. The presumed look-alike was called Mirek and his background stood up. The Security Service calls in Willie 'Glasshouse' Jackson — Jacko — as they realise that there is a more sinister aspect. Jacko and his assistant begin to unearth commercial and political corruption in which life is cheap and profits vast, as the killing machines swing into action.

THE READER

Bernhard Schlink

A schoolboy in post-war Germany, Michael collapses one day in the street and is helped home by a woman in her thirties. He is fascinated by this older woman, and he and Hanna begin a secretive affair. Gradually, he begins to be frustrated by their relationship, but then is shocked when Hanna simply disappears. Some years later, as a law student, Michael is in court to follow a case. To his amazement he recognizes Hanna. The object of his adolescent passion is a criminal. Suddenly, Michael understands that her behaviour, both now and in the past, conceals a deeply buried secret.